YOU ARE OLD ENOUGH SON

Further irreverent recollections of the horror/science fiction/fantasy scene in the British cinema 1971-2005

YOU ARE OLD ENOUGH SON

Further irreverent recollections of the horror/science fiction/fantasy scene in the British cinema 1971-2005

by Barry Atkinson

Midnight Marquee Press, Inc.
Baltimore, MD

Copyright © Barry Atkinson, 2011
Cover Design/Layout Design: Susan Svehla

Without limiting the rights under copyright reserved above, no part of this publication may be reproduced, stored in or introduced into a retrieval system, or transmitted, in any form, or by any means (electronic, mechanical, photocopying, recording or otherwise), without the prior written permission of the copyright owners or the publishers of the book.

ISBN 978-1-936168-13-2
Library of Congress Catalog Card Number 2010938651
Manufactured in the United States of America
First Printing by Midnight Marquee Press, Inc., January 2011

To
Janet

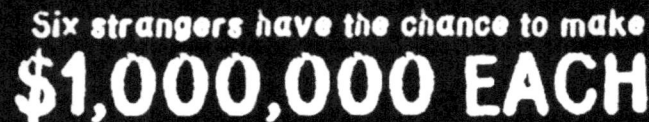

CONTENTS

8	Foreword
9	Chapter One: The Way It Used to Be
12	Chapter Two: 1971-1979
47	Chapter Three: 1980-1989
67	Chapter Four: 1990-1997
88	Chapter Five: An Evening Out—Greek Style (1998)
92	Chapter Six: Highs and Lows (1998-2005)
105	Chapter Seven: That Was Then—This Is Now
111	Chapter Eight: Reflections (2006)
113	Chapter Nine: A Conversation— The Old Versus the New (1)
118	Chapter 10: A Conversation— The Old Versus the New (2)
126	Chapter 11: Postscript

FOREWORD

My previous book on the subject of horror, science fiction, and fantasy films (HSFF): *You're Not Old Enough Son* (Midnight Marquee Press, 2006) chronicled my journeys through the British fantasy cinema scene during the 1950s and 1960s. These were golden years as I viewed them. Years when fantasy fare spanning the decades 1930 to 1960 (but mostly the 1950s) was served up continuously week after week, month after month, and year after year. It was a never-ending supply of goodies to satisfy the most demanding of appetites and mine, it has to be said, was more demanding than most! From a cinematic point of view, those were exciting times, but by the end of 1970, it was all over. Television, to a certain extent, was to blame, as was audience indifference to any film over five years old and made in black and white (the changing face of program presentations). Theaters deemed this too elephantine and old-fashioned to promote an intimate atmosphere required by a modern audience. The movies themselves, style verged between the sublime to the ridiculous combined with innocence, imagination, and pizzazz, all gave way to violence, over-length, and plot-lines sacrificed in the name of million-dollar special effects. To my mind, the sheer naivete, energy, magic, drive, and yes, even the music of the oldies, had vanished and along with it my enthusiasm for the genre. However, all things change, including the 20th century's most popular art-form. Even I realized that an audience in the new decade of the 1970s couldn't (and wouldn't) possibly expect to put up good money to sit through a double bill of *Attack of the Crab Monsters* and *The Beast with a Million Eyes,* which only a few years earlier would have drawn a full house on a rainy Sunday afternoon at Leatherhead's Crescent cinema. Maybe, just maybe, I should join them and stop burying my head in the past, however glorious that past may have been. So I endeavored to put a brave face on things and think more positively—for all one knew, what was around the corner might not be quite as bad as I imagined it to be. These, then, are my continued travels through the fantasy cinema in England from 1971 to 2005. The views on all films mentioned, as in my last book, are entirely my own!

1

THE WAY IT USED TO BE

1954—my introduction began at the tender age of seven to the world of fantasy cinema. Upon exiting The Crescent cinema in Leatherhead I walked up the long dark hill towards home in the blackness of the October night, tightly gripping my mother's hand, trying hard to rid my mind of the disturbing images just encountered in Spartan's hoary old sci-fi potboiler *Devil Girl from Mars*, and knowing full well that several sleepless nights lie in store for me. 1955—shivering in terror at the one-minute trailer to *House of Wax* as Vincent Price's shadow loomed over Phyllis Kirk. 1956—staring in awe at the stills outside The Crescent to *Revenge of the Creature* showing the scaly gill-man up-ending a car and wondering where on earth the flick had come from—not from England, that's for certain. 1957—trembling in fear at the vivid, Eastman-colored one-minute trailer to *The Curse of Frankenstein* as Christopher Lee's shadow hovered horribly over Valerie Gaunt. 1958—leafing slowly through the pages of Forrest J Ackerman's legendary horror magazine, *Famous Monsters of Filmland*, eyes on stalks, scaring myself and my mates silly as one hideous creature, monster, vampire, werewolf, mutation, dinosaur, giant insect, and alien after another met our startled gazes. They ingrained themselves deep into the subconscious regions of our minds. 1959—being thrown unceremoniously out of the despicable Crescent after unsuccessfully attempting, two years short of the proper age in the United Kingdom, to see the A-rated *The Amazing Colossal Man*. 1960—sneaking into The Crescent with more than a little help from my father to catch Hammer's *The Mummy*, which was my introduction to the world of the adult horror film and my first "X" picture. Being two and a three quarter years under the legal age in England (which then was 16) to sit through such a film and reveling in the experience. 1961—gawping in amazement at the colorful stills to *Rodan* outside the still-impregnable Crescent, wishing fervently I could be inside watching it. To make up for this disappointment, I successfully, at the age of 14, negotiated the ticket barrier at Dorking's Embassy and caught my first pair of American "X" classified horror movies: *The Creature Walks Among Us* coupled with *Tarantula*. 1962—sitting among a transfixed full house in Dorking's Embassy cinema, I was glued to a double "X" bill of *I Was A Teenage Werewolf* and *It Conquered the World*, which were the first of dozens of tremendous horror double bills which I caught that year on the all-conquering Sunday one-day circuit. 1963—in Cornwall, studying the local paper and trying to decide whether to see *Monster on the Campus* and *The Land Unknown* at the ABC in Falmouth, *The Fiend Who Walked the West* and *The Unknown Terror* at the Odeon in Falmouth, *Seddok, Son of Satan* and *Frantic* at The Regal in Redruth, *Cult of the Cobra* and *Curse of the Undead* at The Flora

Patricia Laffan as Nyah, *The Devil Girl from Mars*.

in Helston, or *The Tingler* and *The H-Man* at The Palace in Truro. I wondered if my meager pocket money could stretch to two showings in two days. 1964—*The Gargon Terror* and *Gigantis the Fire Monster*, *The Monster of Piedras Blancas* and *The Dead One,* and *The Black Scorpion* and *Macabre*—three double "X" bills seen within the space of a week; 1965—trying hard to concentrate on *The Diabolical Dr. Satan* in a ramshackle cinema on the outskirts of Piraeus, Greece, surrounded by small children and chickens, with most of the picture projected onto the crumbling ceiling. 1966—*House of Wax* and *Phantom of the Rue Morgue*, *The Curse of Frankenstein* and *Dracula*, Hammer's *The Mummy* and *The Brides of Dracula*, *The Man Who Could Cheat Death* and *The Blob*. The re-issues begin, while *Curse of the Undead* and *The Thing that Couldn't Die* at Falmouth's ABC in December signal the virtual end to the Sunday one-day programs. 1967—*King Kong* and *The Thing from Another World*, *Psycho* and *The War of the Worlds*, *Mysterious Island*, Lugosi's *Dracula* and *Creature from the Black Lagoon*, *The Birds* and *The Day of the Triffids*, *The Beast from*

20,000 Fathoms, Jason and the Argonauts, The Pit and the Pendulum and *The Premature Burial*. These reissues continue unabated. 1968—I was straining to stay awake during a late-night presentation of Universal's *The Deadly Mantis* and *The Land Unknown* at Redhill's giant Odeon, emerging into the night air at two in the morning, feeling sick, and nauseous. 1969—staving off bouts of tiredness during another midnight show, this time *Kiss of the Vampire* and *Tarantula* were playing at the ABC in Falmouth. 1970—a rewarding late-night double "X" presentation of *Psycho* and *Bride of Frankenstein* at The Regal in Redruth, which was the last late show of its type I ever attended without realizing it at the time.

Between 1954 and 1970, over 400 films belonging to the HSFF genre passed before my eyes, a great many of them several times over. What would the ensuing decade come up with that could possibly equal those incredibly fruitful, productive, and, yes, fabulous 16 years? Turn the pages to find out!

2

1971-1979

If the period between 1954 and 1970 had symbolized the peak years in terms of fantasy film viewing on an unprecedented scale in England, then 1971, kicking off the new decade, represented a nadir of sorts. The Sunday one-day programs had been a fertile breeding ground in the early to mid-1960s for fantasy fodder of every conceivable shape, size, and (occasionally) color were long gone. And the late-night shows, similarly productive in screening a wealth of great HSFF presentations, had trickled to a halt. No more vintage black-and-white delights from the 1930s, 1940s, and 1950s were being shown in the U.K.'s cinemas. Even the output of the 1960s (not in the same league as the previous three decades, but nevertheless containing some gems amid the dross) had mysteriously disappeared. Television, after a brief burst of activity during the latter part of 1968 and continuing through 1969 when quite a few horror, science fiction, and fantasy classics were given a first-ever airing, had decided, in all of its questionable wisdom, that the genre perhaps did not command a big enough audience (in the United Kingdom, that is) to justify constant showings on the networks. Out of the 122 movies I caught on the box in 1971, only a paltry 11 were fantasy—*Journey to the Center of the Earth, The Birds, The Hunchback of Notre Dame* (1939), *Forbidden Planet, The Seventh Voyage of Sinbad, She* (1965), *Mysterious Island, On the Beach, Captain Sinbad, The Time Machine,* and *Things to Come*. As if that wasn't bad enough, the influence of the censor's office, that had held sway over the cinema throughout the previous four decades, handing out first the "H" and then the "X" and "A" certificates here, there and everywhere, exerted itself on those selfsame films that were now appearing on the small screen. This, combined with the commercial station's irritating practice of fitting movies into the all-important time slot and an allowance for the dreaded adverts, meant that many HSFF pictures were broadcast both on BBC and ITV in a truncated form—every one of the aforementioned 11 movies had been edited for television viewing. *The Seventh Voyage of Sinbad* was screened in its 1964 severely cut incarnation and not the complete 1958 version. *Forbidden Planet* had several key scenes missing, which chiefly were in the last 20 minutes where none of the Krel's underground machinery was shown. Hitchcock's *The Birds* omitted most of the bloody attack by our feathered friends on Tippi Hedren. Charles Laughton's magnificent Quasimodo was notable by his absence for a lot of the time. The worst hit, though, was *Journey to the Center of the Earth,* shorn by at least 35 minutes—a 132-minute classic reduced to 97 minutes. This act of butchery had me firing off a letter of protest to the highbrow but eminently readable *Films and Filming* magazine who were waging a war against certain regional television companies' mishandling of movies in general, but I wasn't alone in venting my anger and frustration at the commercial channel's (the main culprit) clumsy and unfeeling treatment of certain pictures—others had already written in to complain as well, in droves.

My letter, which was published by the magazine, read:

Dear Sirs,

I am writing to you in disgust regarding the screening of the 20th Century Fox fantasy *Journey to the Center of The Earth* which was shown on ITV on Saturday, June 26 at 5:15 p.m. to 7:00 p.m. The film's original running time was 132 minutes, whereby allowing for adverts between the 105-minute time slot allocated for the movie, you were left with a total length of 97 minutes, which meant that several crucial sequences essential for the first-time viewer to follow the threads of the storyline were missing. Noticeably the following threads were missing:

1) All explanations as to how Professor James Mason discovers the cryptic message to the Earth's center was gone— you jumped from the opening shots in the Edinburgh streets to the preparations for the journey itself.

2) The intrepid explorers line up on the crater's edge to begin their descent and are next seen running from a rather large boulder. The actual descent and the initial scenes inside the volcanic crater had been edited out.

3) The complete crystal grotto segment was nowhere to be seen.

4) Several skips in the lengthy footage showing a lost Pat Boone searching desperately for his comrades indicated more scissor-work.

5) The mock trial for murder of Count Saknussemm and parts of the lost city of the Atlantis climax towards the end was absent.

By my estimation, almost 35 minutes have been cut from the original print. This is a deplorable state of affairs, but one that many a film fan has come to expect from this company. In its present state, the film isn't worth watching at all. I sincerely hope that your campaign to prevent such wholesale carving-up of movies by the various commercial stations has some effect in the future, which is to prevent this kind of thing from happening time and time again.

Yours faithfully...

Nothing, I contemplated, had changed—*Psycho* had been shown with several small edits at the end of 1968. For this eagle-eyed viewer, this was easily spotted. *Behemoth the Sea Monster* was the A-rated version, which was not the original "X" picture. *The Beast from 20,000 Fathoms* was shorter by at least eight minutes (I astutely timed it!) and even the odd Hammer production had been trimmed for public consumption (despite being stuck on at a very late hour). Where would it all end, I thought despondently? What was the point in putting these films on in an abridged form? They might just as well be left alone until such time as Britain's rigorous censorship laws relaxed a bit—whenever that might be.

The cinema scene was just as depressing—seven HSFF movies over a 12-month period. Hell, not so long ago, I could notch up that number in a week! And six out of the seven didn't exactly set the screen alight. *I, Monster, Countess Dracula, The Vampire Lovers, Eye of the Cat, The Dunwich Horror,* and *Blood on Satan's Claw*—routine outings (each and every one of them) and Hammer's output, I noticed, was veering more and more towards sex, nudity, and titillation than out-and-out flamboyant horror. This was a gradual decline in comparison to their earlier high-caliber efforts. The seventh, Douglas Trumbull's *Silent Running*, fell firmly into the category that this movie could have been a whole lot better. Employing many of the sets and models featured in Kubrick's *2001*, on which Trumbull worked as a special effects supervisor, the story told of a vast eco-ship drifting in space run by Bruce Dern and his robot assistants. This was a Garden of Eden intended to replenish a war-ravaged Earth. Ridiculously short for a film of this scope and concept (89 minutes) and also bereft of any narrative drive, *Silent Running* meandered all over the place. In spite of its spectacular visuals, it remained strangely unsatisfying, as though cobbled together as an afterthought when Kubrick had finally completed work on his groundbreaking masterpiece.

I was back living in Cornwall later that year and it was crystal clear to me that even my once all-time favorite cinema, The Cameo in Lower Roskear, had seemingly given up on the oldies. Instead, they concentrated on continental sex fare and the newer releases, although *Kiss of the Vampire, The Pit and the Pendulum,* Toho's original *Godzilla, Blood and Black Lace,* and *Creature from the Black Lagoon* all put in an appearance—otherwise occupied at the time, I missed them all.

1972 forced me to realize that things were never going to be as they once were. So I might just as well get used to it. On television, out of 98 films seen, the HSFF ratio was still poor—a miserly 16, including the butchered print of *Journey to the Center of the Earth* screened for a second time. Obviously, the letters of complaint to *Films and Filming* magazine concerning the shoddy state of this sumptuous fantasy adventure had fallen on the television network's deaf ears. I had now returned to the Redhill area of Surrey (I won't try to explain this backward and forwarding between Surrey and Cornwall. It's far too complicated!), Redhill's Odeon, together with Reigate's Majestic and Hippodrome, my three local cinemas, and London only a half hour's journey away by train, the West End's plethora of splendiferous cinemas and multitude of smaller theaters on the Capital's outskirts provided both size and comfort, but at a cost. Among other things, the year was notable for the release of three features which gave the still-strict British film censor an almighty headache—*A Clockwork Orange, The Devils,* and *Straw Dogs.* Much as Hammer had done during the 1950s, breaking every kind of filmic taboo in the book with a string of X-rated horror movies. These films tested the censor's patience to extreme limits. All three contained scenes guaranteed to have the censor's office staff reaching for their overworked scissors while getting extremely hot under the collar—rape and violence, both bloody and cold, together with full-frontal nudity. In the long run, it was left to the local authorities to decide whether or not to screen these films in their respective areas, and in what form. Consequently,

Ken Russell's *The Devils* was banned in large parts of England—I caught it at The King's cinema in Camborne, Cornwall. Although too hysterical and overwrought for my liking, the film was an "X" in every sense of the word. The gross-out climax, whereby Oliver Reed is burnt at the stake after his legs have been broken, left me with a sick feeling in the pit of my stomach. Wasn't anything sacred anymore, I mused? Everything had to be overstated—nothing was left to the imagination, which was a trend that would continue and escalate alarmingly over the ensuing years. Sam Peckinpah's *Straw Dogs*, which was filmed on Cornwall's far southwest coast and similarly banned in many counties, was shown, for obvious reasons, in Cornwall. This film certified an X-rating and was a rather tacky and unexceptional potboiler. Despite the big names behind it, it culminated in a savage climax: Dustin Hoffman defended his cottage, by various brutal means, against a gang of murderous villagers all lusting after (and who could blame them) his wife Susan George.

The most controversial of the trio was Stanley Kubrick's *A Clockwork Orange*, which was banned outright in Surrey. To see for myself what all the fuss and commotion was about over this particular picture, I traveled up to London to sit in a packed house at the luxurious Warner Theater. Personally, I reckoned that Malcolm McDowell was the bee's knees as the depraved, swaggering, and ultra-violent Alex and surely deserved an Oscar nomination, although *A Clockwork Orange* was definitely *not* the kind of movie to be featured or mentioned at the Oscar ceremonies, however brilliant the direction and vision in translating Anthony Burgess' most infamous novel to the silver screen was. The critics and the censor were outraged at the three rape scenes included in the first 45 minutes and the dispassionate use of aggressive images, while secretly applauding the director for producing at least something a bit more powerful than most of the fodder they had to sit through and judge. The critics even perhaps acknowledged that the film would turn out to be quite influential for many reasons. But despite my affections for this deranged youth, I

certainly didn't return home and buy myself a white boiler suit, boots, and a bowler hat, then go out on a rampage as did thousands of other juveniles in the country, who all acted out the film's nastier elements. This formed an army of droogs on the march bent on creating mayhem and havoc—this was one of the main reasons why the director decided to withdraw his most notorious piece of work from circulation a year later. The reputation it gained brought about its eventual downfall. It would not be released again in the United Kingdom (even on VHS and DVD) until 2000 where it would resurface with an "18" certificate. (Note: In 1991, it was rumored that BBC2 television was considering screening *A Clockwork Orange* at midnight on a Saturday with extensive cuts to appease both the censor's office and the British Broadcasting Corporation's own code of conduct. Luckily, a carved-up print of Kubrick's classic never made it onto the small screen. It wasn't until 2002 that the movie was premiered on the box. The more liberal-minded Channel 4 broadcast the film in its entirety.)

Apart from the three aforementioned movies, there wasn't a great deal more on offer out on the circuits to get the juices flowing. Hammer's latest double horror bill: *Dr. Jekyll and Sister Hyde* coupled with *Blood from the Mummy's Tomb*, went the rounds and both were typical as straightforward horror fare of the day. But the company's fertile years of 1955 through 1963 seemed an awful long way back in terms of panache and imaginative production design and color. *Vampire Circus* summed up the company's current output to a tee. A vampire count threatens retribution on a village that condemned him to eternal death. His acolytes man a circus that enters the village—very soon, the villagers are dying one by one in a most gruesome manner. Finally, after several vampirisms, the young hero rescues the heroine and decapitates the reactivated count as he is about to start a new reign of terror. Flatly directed by Robert Young, the film had muddy photography, an ear-blasting and totally nondescript soundtrack, and enough bare breasts on display to satisfy the dirty raincoat brigade. It all contributed to a very middle-of-the-road vampire flick that had little merit in its 87-minute running time. Worse still was *Dracula AD 1972*, which was the second-to-last in Hammer's *Dracula* franchise. Running out of ideas as to what to do next with the old bloodsucker, some bright spark at the studio must have come up with the lame idea of introducing the Count to swinging London. The end result turned out to be a parody of the vampire legend, whereby Lee appears silent and embarrassed throughout, and an older-looking Cushing as a descendant of Van Helsing is trying to terminate the vampire's reign as numerous nubile young women experience vampirism in bloody fashion. The usual fight-to-the-death climax was its one saving grace. Even so, *Dracula AD 1972* remains the poorest of Hammer's *Dracula* series by a long run.

Meanwhile, Amicus, a smallish independent company attempting to give the off-form Hammer a run for their money, released two more of its lively horror compendiums: *Tales from the Crypt* and *Asylum*. Steven Spielberg's giant killer truck-on-the-loose thriller, *Duel,* introduced me to Britain's latest certificate, the AA. In 1971, the British film ratings of U (for all), A (14 and over; under if accompanied by an adult) and X (16 and over) were upgraded to U (for all), A (five and over), AA (15 and over) and X (18 and over). In other words, there were four ratings to contend with instead of three. Fair enough, the new X pictures were a damn sight more graphic and gorier than the older ones, although they lacked overall quality in most areas apart from Kubrick's *tour de force,* which I dragged a mate of mine along to see at The Warner in London—speculation was rife in the press that it was going to be withdrawn from U.K. cinemas very shortly because of the trouble it was causing among the nation's disaffected youth. Due to this fact, I wanted to experience it again before it disappeared from sight. So one day in July, I telephoned Robert in Ashtead: "Fancy going up to London on Saturday?"

"Yes, OK. What do you plan on doing?"

"Buy a few records and take in *A Clockwork Orange* for a second look. It's a real hoot. I think you'll like it."

"Oh." He didn't appear all that keen in my choice of celluloid entertainment, which was not like the old gang of yesteryear who couldn't wait to see such fare and sounded bloody enthusiastic about it.

"Right. Meet you at Victoria Station around midday then."

Later on Saturday afternoon, we left the cinema, joined the crowds thronging Leicester Square, and I turned to Robert for an opinion.

"Well? What do you reckon on that?"

He sniffed. "Not bad—a bit long, though. To be perfectly frank, it's not really my taste in films."

In other words, the United Kingdom's most reviled (in some quarters) and talked-about picture had failed to make an impact. I was a tad unhappy at his remark, but then remembered that this wasn't the year 1962. The year when hordes of cinema-mad customers queued up round the block, who eagerly anticipated the Sunday presentation of *The Mummy's Ghost* double billed with *Frankenstein Meets the Wolf Man.* This included me and my little band of fantasy-addicted warriors. No, this was 1972, being 10 long years later. Times had changed—we had all grown up and supposedly moved on. The "having a good time" element was no longer there or the appreciation of what was on offer. Now it was a case of seeing one film one week, be it in Redhill, Reigate, or in London, and then waiting in vain for the next delight to appear. Unfortunately, there wasn't an abundance of HSFF movies—it was slim pickings amid the likes of *Dirty Harry, The Godfather,* and *The French Connection,* which were outstanding feature films in their own right admittedly, but not belonging to my favored genre.

At the end of 1972, American International released *The Abominable Dr. Phibes* with *Dr. Phibes Rises Again,* these films are two worthy efforts starring Vincent Price in what he was the undisputed master of—high-camp, ghoulish black humor within a horror context. The first of the duo was a cross between *The Phantom of the Opera* and *House of Wax*, with Price as the disfigured doctor dispatching those who were unable to save his wife's life in a surgical operation. His inspiration behind the deaths stemmed from the 10 plagues of Egypt in the Old Testament. In the sequel, the mad doctor sets about restoring his wife with the aid of a mute assistant and bumping off his enemies by suitably macabre methods. But these new double horror bills were not the draws they once were—a half-empty Odeon in Redhill testified to the waning influence of both this school of horror movie and the presentation. Customers' tastes were now gravitating towards violent gangster and detective thrillers with the lumbering disaster variety of motion picture (*The Poseidon Adventure*, *The Towering Inferno*) just around the corner to push HSFF further back into the shadows.

Japanese poster for *Solaris*

A high-quality, though perplexing, sci-fi outing from this period was the Russian space epic *Solaris*, which was touted in the papers as the Soviets' answer to *2001: A Space Odyssey*. The film ran 167 minutes in length and was "thought provoking" in the words of one critic, whose words would have me checking out the movie under review. The film was denied a general release because the main distributors in the United Kingdom tended to shy away from foreign movies. In their eyes, they deemed the movies not good box office material. When I went up to London to take in the mind-boggling cinematic event, it was short on *2001*-type effects, but just as enigmatic. Concerning the crew of a space station, they had fallen prey to the mysterious living planet beneath them, which functioned as a conscience to their hopes and fears. Intellectually challenging, I could understand why *Solaris* would never appeal to a mass audience, for much of it was very slow-moving, talkative, and with subtitles to match, but I appreciated it as something of a cut above the usual fare. Unfortunately even in those days, prices in London were a great deal higher than in the provinces and it cost me an arm and a leg to see the film.

One of the very last of the classier Hammer double bills appeared towards the end of the year: *Hands of the Ripper* and *Twins of Evil*. *Ripper* was yet another retelling of the Jack the Ripper legend. This time the film starred Angharad Rees as the serial killer's daughter. She committed a series of murders whilst in a trance-like state. Eric Porter plays a psychiatrist who attempts, unsuccessfully, to unravel her mind, which eventually leads to his death and hers. It was well directed by Peter Sasdy and nattier than the average horror movie, which included *Twins of Evil* that involved the real-life Collinson twins. One portrayed a vampire and the other the damsel in distress. They were at the mercy of puritanical Peter Cushing in *Witchfinder General* mode. Moderately successful at the box office, Hammer seemed to have pushed the boat out on these two. What came after (with the odd exception) didn't really match up. The company gradually drifted down the road to artistic and financial oblivion, their demise, some would say, was quickened by their foray into television one-hour specials such as the *Hammer House of Horrors* series shown in the early 1980s.

Back on television, Nigel Kneale's *The Stone Tape* would have made a superb motion picture and an ideal vehicle, perhaps, for Hammer. As it was, the BBC screened it as a 90-minute special. It was a terrifying tale concerning a group of scientists moving into a renovated mansion. Inside, one gloomy room remains unfinished due to the fact that the builders refuse to work there. Very soon, the scientists encounter a ghostly force within the room itself. It leads to a tragic climax when Jane Asher (who, out of the group, is the member most susceptible to paranormal activity) becomes a victim of the malevolent manifestations which have lurked there for centuries. Repeated in 1973 and not seen for over 30 years, this remains one of Kneale's most accomplished essays in supernatural horror outside of his celebrated *Quatermass* trilogy of the 1950s.

For me, 1973 was the worst year cinema-wise since I first trotted into the Astoria theater in Farnham in 1951 at the age of four to see Disney's *Cinderella*—a solitary one film, Clint Eastwood's violent X-rated *High Plains Drifter*, a pseudo-Western sporting mystical elements within its framework (a taciturn Eastwood is an avenging demon-type figure) and a pretty good flick of its type, was modeled on his *Dollar* trilogy. The film was stylishly put together, brutal, and very cool. There literally wasn't anything else to be had out there or nothing that I was especially interested in. On the television front, the tally was a disappointing 26 HSFF pictures out of a total of 117 seen, the highlight was a beautifully restored print of *Mystery of the Wax Museum*, screened in two-tone Technicolor at the unearthly hour of midnight. The TV bosses reasoned that some kids might still be awake fairly late, but not that late (yes, even a horror film made as far back as 1933 could cause censorship problems on the small screen!). It's a pity that video recorders were not available in those days. So it was a case of once seen, now more or less forgotten. As for the others, the television companies were simply broadcasting the same old product over and over again with nothing new on the horizon—*Forbidden Planet, Jason and the Argonauts, On the Beach, Journey to the Center of the Earth* (the chopped-up print), and *The Time Machine*. Surely there was a limit, even to a fanatic such as myself, as to how many times you could sit through these delights before becoming immune to their undoubted charms.

Max von Sydow, Jason Miller and Linda Blair in *The Exorcist*

After the dire 1973, 1974 could only be an improvement. It was, despite the latest cinematic craze to grab the public's attention, which were martial arts movies. Sandwiched between Bruce Lee's trio of atrociously dubbed and beat-them-up brand of "X" features: *Big Boss, Fists of Fury,* and *Enter the Dragon*, were such treats (although I use the term loosely here) as *Westworld, The Exorcist, The Golden Voyage of Sinbad,* and Hammer's latest offering, *Frankenstein and the Monster from Hell*. The latter was a recovery of sorts to the company's former glories and it stood head and shoulders above their previous three *Frankenstein* pictures. It was created by reuniting an aging, grizzled, but still authoritarian Peter Cushing with Terence Fisher, who was coaxed out of semi-retirement to direct this rather cold and clinical final entry in the long-running series. Reminiscent in many ways of a 1960s continental surgical/horror movie, Fisher provided a much-needed expert touch to the proceedings. The ape-like monster looked suitably malformed and the asylum setting was expertly devised as well. Cushing's black-hearted Baron was the doctor attending to the inmates of an asylum. Aided by Shane Briant and Madeline Smith, the doctor transplanted a professor's brain into a hulking brute of a creature with disastrous results. With a half-decent score provided by veteran composer James Bernard, gruesome laboratory sequences that didn't look out of place in the gore/slasher movies that were about to burst upon the scene, and a sharp script, *Frankenstein and the Monster from Hell* harked back, in some respects, to the Gothic splendor of *The Curse of Frankenstein* and remains a much underrated picture in the Hammer stable. Teamed up with Shaw's X-rated *Fists of Vengeance*, this was one of the year's better double "X" programs and a temporary return to form for England's once illustrious producers of top quality horror fare.

On the other hand, *Captain Kronos: Vampire Hunter* was yet another desperate attempt by Hammer to revitalize their flagging run of vampire tales. Directed and produced by British TV comedy specialist Brian Clemens, it told of a blond caped soldier and his two assistants who battled a female vampire in a remote village where young women succumbed rather quickly to premature aging. Originally scheduled for release in 1972, but delayed for two years, this was a jumble of ideas and styles that verged from campy horror to comedy and it didn't work at all. Together with the co-feature, *Fear in the Night*, a latter-day Hammer psychodrama that was short on suspense, even though the reliable Peter Cushing was involved, it showed that the company was struggling to come up with a formula that even remotely resembled that incredibly productive period from 1955 to 1963, which was the classic heyday of Hammer as I and many others termed it.

I thought it was high time that my four-year-old son was introduced to the world of the cinema and what better film to introduce him to than a fantasy feature: *The Golden Voyage of Sinbad*, which was Ray Harryhausen's latest concoction after a lengthy lay-off of five-odd years. Against the wishes of my wife, who stated "He's far too young to be watching stuff like that and he'll get nightmares," I took Stephen along to the spacious Redhill Odeon to the early afternoon Saturday show. Unfortunately, I should have taken heed of my wife's words. For even though I timed the visit so that we skipped the adverts, missed the trailers, and sat down as the heavy red curtains quickly rolled back over the opening credits, Stephen remained singularly unimpressed by the first 20 minutes. Instead, his attention was focused, much to their annoyance and mine, on the people trying to enjoy Sinbad's adventures behind us. He fidgeted in his seat and the whole cinema experience went right over his head. After 25 minutes, I had enough and gave up. I was concentrating too much on Stephen's antics and not what I had paid good money for, so I gathered up my troublesome toddler and beat a hasty retreat. Several hours later, I returned on my own to catch the seven o'clock performance.

And what did I think of Columbia's brand-new Dynamation offering? Much like the latter-day Hammer movies, this latter-day *Sinbad* outing wasn't a patch on the original, which in this case, was *The Seventh Voyage of Sinbad*. The color was drab, the action and direction rather plodding, the monsters were so-so, but not really standing out as such (think Cyclops and Talos and you'll get my drift), and there was no Bernard Herrmann score to drive it along. The sparkle, the razzle-dazzle, and the sheer novelty factor of the effects were mostly absent, although the production was entertaining enough and any Harryhausen fantasy was an event in itself, especially in the hard-nosed atmosphere of the 1970s.

The Seventh Voyage of Sinbad boasted a great Bernard Herrmann score and dazzling creatures.

Later, I returned home and tried to interest Stephen in what he had missed out on, but it fell on stony ground—he didn't appear to be a fledgling fantasy fan at the moment.

In July, I took my wife along to Reigate's Majestic to catch the current movie upsetting the British censor. It was William Friedkin's blood and thunder exercise in demonic possession: *The Exorcist*, which was banned from several counties, criticized by umpteen religious groups, and had reports of fainting in the cinemas that were allowed to screen it. I sat among a packed house as the ghastly and very noisy shenanigans unfolded before us. An hour or so into the film, my wife excused herself to go to the toilet. She quickly returned and whispered to me in the darkness.

"Guess what. There are three girls in there being sick."

"What? Because of this?" I whispered back. Blimey, it wasn't all that bad, surely.

"Yes," she confirmed. "I couldn't pay a penny. The cubicles are all full."

During the remainder of the picture, four more females decided that repeated shots of Linda Blair vomiting green slime over all and sundry was too much to bear and scooted out of the auditorium in great haste. Me? *The Exorcist* was undeniably well-produced and contained a few hair-raising scenes calculatedly devised to jolt and shock a modern-day audience. This included the exorcism climax in which Friedkin threw in everything but the kitchen sink. However, my mind still had a habit of comparing the new with the old and it was no better or more frightening than, say, 1963's *The Haunting*, despite all of its pyrotechnics and Blair's hideous makeup job. It seemed to me that the contemporary paying customer had to be hit over the head with a sledgehammer in order to appreciate these newer horror films—subtle it certainly wasn't, yet crude it certainly was.

After another somewhat unremarkable double "X" bill, which paired *The Ghoul* with *The Fiend*, which were two dreadfully flat features that had me leaving the ABC Croydon in despair at the current state of such fodder, I took in Hammer's final *Dracula* outing: *The Satanic Rites of Dracula* a week later, paired with Tigon's *The Creeping Flesh*. *Satanic Rites* marked the end of the Lee/Cushing vampire partnership (Cushing played Van Helsing's descendant one more time in *The Legend of the Seven Golden Vampires*, which I didn't catch) and it ended on a whimper. Again, the up-to-date setting jarred and the intriguing storyline could have been better developed. In the film, Dracula planned to destroy mankind with a bacteriological virus created by scientist Freddie Jones and Cushing's daughter was kidnapped and held captive in the vampire's country retreat. This was a total lack of flair that highlighted Hammer's final throw of the *Dracula* dice. The two old foes simply went through the motions, which brought about a sad ending to a series that had degenerated alarmingly over the past few years. To compensate for this, *The Creeping Flesh*, a film about a giant prehistoric skeleton that comes alive after scientist Peter Cushing tips moisture over one of its severed fingers, was far more inventive. It was almost a *menage a trois* as Cushing is imprisoned by his mad brother, Christopher Lee, and leaves his wife and daughter to be tormented by him. The cloaked and putrefying skeleton is left to roam the bleak countryside slaying all those who encounter it. Like Amicus, Tigon, another of the smaller British independents, turned out a fair number of horror movies during the '70s. Taking up the Hammer mantle with some degree of critical, if not commercial, success, *The Creeping Flesh* was one of their smarter efforts, which benefitted from Freddie Francis' imaginative direction.

John Hough, who had directed the commendable *Twins of Evil*, came unstuck with *The Legend of Hell House*, a muddled adaptation of Richard Matheson's best-selling novel, which concerned a group of psychics investigating a series of haunting moments in a remote mansion. After an encouraging start, the film ran out of steam and degenerated into a number of ghostly set pieces, which were clumsily handled. The walled-up corpse of the mansion's mad former owner was the culprit behind the visitations from beyond the grave. The dimly lit photography and unsatisfactory climax all added up to a substandard variation on MGM's *The Haunting*, which still was the Number One film among haunted mansion movies.

A much more rewarding double bill was Tod Browning's 1932 *Freaks* teamed up with Erle C. Kenton's little-seen *Island of Lost Souls*. London pos-

Christopher Lee in the final Dracula outing from Hammer, *The Satanic Rites of Dracula.*

sessed a wealth of extravagant cinemas, but also hundreds of smaller venues, many of them were tucked away from the Capital's main commercial center and situated inside streets well away from the crowds. Combing the *London Evening Standard*, one could sometimes track down, with a little perseverance, a tremendous oldie, one that had long disappeared from the circuits, but which had been resurrected by some enterprising individual who still placed a value on whatever he (or she) chose to present to the public. It was one such evening in October that I was casually browsing through the entertainments section of the paper when I spotted this double bill. One which would have graced The Cameo in Cornwall or The Embassy in Dorking on a Sunday afternoon many moons ago. Under the title "The Movies They Dared To Ban!" the Classic down the Old Kent Road was screening two 1932 horror treats, both of which had received long bans in Britain. *Freaks* had received a 30-year ban and *Island of Lost Souls* was barred from our shores for 26 years. Both were now classified "X" despite their age. Any prior arrangements I had for the coming Saturday were blotted from my mind. This was one double bill I was not going to miss out on because of it being screened for a limited time only.

It was a lengthy trek to reach this cinema, involving a train, tube, and a 30-minute footslog at the end of it. The theater, when I eventually reached it, was a dive and a real bug-hut. Its frayed art-deco interior smelled of disinfectant, there were around 20 old-looking customers settling themselves down into lumpy seats as *Island of Lost Souls* flickered up on the smallish screen, and the print was in fair condition considering the vintage nature of the celluloid. Charles Laughton was superb as the bulky, sweating, and rolling-eyed doctor keeping his experimental animal-people in check with his whip and Lugosi hamming it up as the Speaker of the Law. The delirious climax saw Laughton being dragged off to the House of Pain by his creations. I could see why the British authorities had banned it all those years ago. Vivisection was a forbidden subject in the eyes of the censor (as were blood transfusion-related topics) and the content of *Island of Lost Souls* was considered too strong for a 1930s audience. (Apparently author H.G. Wells was delighted at the ban—he hated the film.)

After the trailers and adverts, it was the turn of *Freaks*, a powerful exercise in utter bizarreness. It included the unreal, unnatural, freaky, and unique in the annals of cinema by allowing real aberrations of nature to be cast as themselves (a bearded lady, dwarves, an armless and legless man, and the pin-headed woman). The print was scratchy, had a habit of jumping every few minutes, and the sound muted by modern standards, but this didn't detract from the weirdness of it all. The final scenes showed Olga Baclanova transformed into a grotesque chicken-woman by the freaks, in revenge for her attempt to poison her dwarf husband, which was oddly disturbing, even after a period of 42 years. When I left the cinema at five o'clock in the afternoon, I was glad that I had made the effort to see this program. For making the long journey back to home seemed a bit more palatable. *Freaks* was shown on British television in 1977, but hasn't been broadcast since then.

(Note: *You're Not Old Enough Son*: Chapter 20 page 123 omits this pairing of two golden greats seen between 1971 and 2003. With 52 years worth of paraphernalia lying around in boxes together with diaries, reams of notes, articles, and a memory that can only hold so much, items were bound to get overlooked and this was one of them. Therefore, I unashamedly apologize to all readers of the first book!)

The scene on television had perked up at last—91 films were seen, a whopping 34 of which were fantasy, and at long last the first transmission of one of Universal's classic *Frankenstein* movies—*Son of Frankenstein*, followed a week later by *House of Wax* and a week after that *The Curse of Frankenstein*. All were broadcast uncut, which was fine by me. The downside, though, was that any film that had been granted an "X" certificate for cinema release was more often than not shown late at night, which was from around 11:00 p.m. and usually at midnight. It was incorrectly assumed that children and people of a nervous disposition were asleep at this ungodly hour. The video recorder was still a few years off so many nights were spent on the sofa, straining to stay awake, and staving off sleep until the early hours of the morning. Not sharing my passion for these old gems, my wife retired to bed hours earlier. In fact, the late-night shows were revisited—on the box! What was the upshot of this? A thumping head the following morning and no sympathetic noises from my partner.

Out of 114 movies seen on the small screen in 1975, 31 were HSFF and most of them were included in a BBC2 Saturday night feature entitled *Midnight Movie Fantastic,* which ran for several weeks, commenced at (yes, you've guessed it) midnight, and transmitted through to the wee small hours as two films were paired up. Double "X" and "A" programs now screened on television instead of at a cinema on a Sunday or presented as a late-night attraction at the nearest Odeon. How times had changed! Still, one couldn't complain and some of the billings were quite creatively put together—*Quatermass 2* followed by *The Abominable Snowman*, the 1919 *The Cabinet of Dr. Caligari* with *X the Unknown,* and *Metropolis* coupled with Hammer's *The Man Who Could Cheat Death*. A video recorder would have come in handy during this non-VHS period as I staggered bleary-eyed to bed at three in the morning and my head throbbing with the beginnings of a migraine, but that was the law of the land—adult fare such as this had to go out at a very late hour of the day, come what may. That, apparently, was the dictate from those on high responsible for such things.

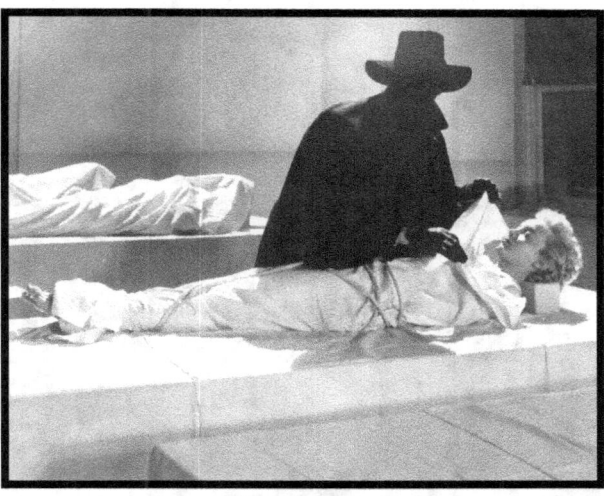

House of Wax

At the London Film Festival, the latest shocker from across the Atlantic was given an airing, *The Texas Chain Saw Massacre*, and I, along with legions of horror fans, eagerly awaited its release onto the local circuits, but we waited in vain. The grandfather of the splatter/dismembered limbs category of movie fell victim to the stringent British censorship laws and was refused a certificate (although it was secretly shown on the underground circuit). Yet in hindsight, it was no more disturbing than many of the sadistic exploitation continental pictures of the '60s, '70s and even some of the meatier Hammer films. So this unrelenting and amateurishly shot B picture concerning chainsaw-wielding Leather-face and his gang of cannibalistic retards tormenting and slaughtering a family had to wait another 20 years or so before seeing the light of day (legally, that is) in Britain. On the opposite end of the scales to *The Texas Chain Saw*

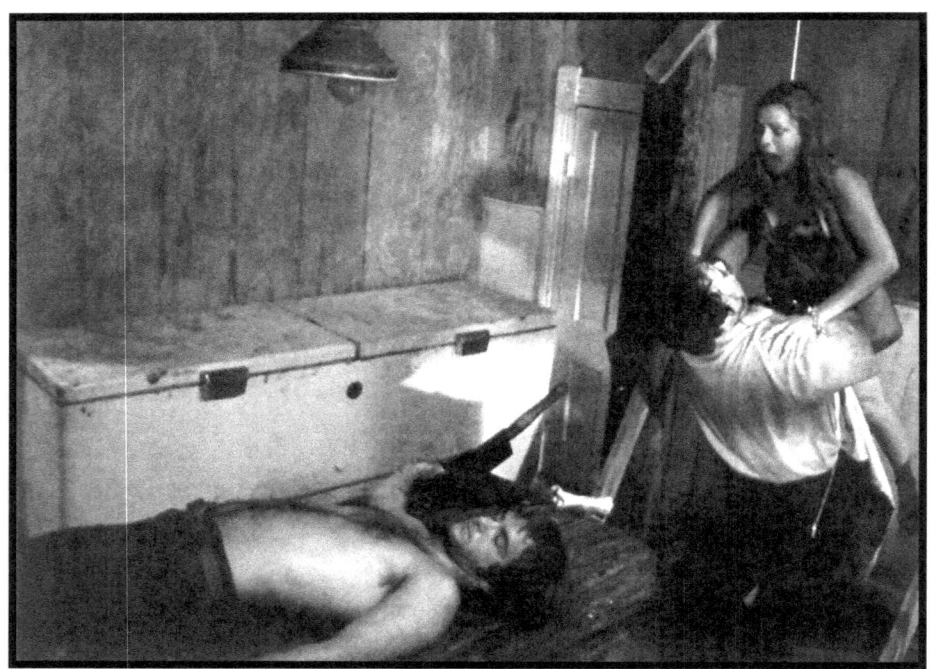

Texas Chain Saw Massacre

Massacre was Peter Weir's leisurely paced *Picnic at Hanging Rock*. This was a haunting Australian fantasy, which was not given a national outing. So another day out in London was called for because the film played at various art-house venues in the city. It was a strange tale of a group of schoolgirls in 1900 who disappear when exploring rock formations in the Outback. The movie had a great many underlying sexual symbolic messages built into its 115 minutes, but remained as an absorbing journey into the mysterious, the puzzling, and was beautifully photographed in soft-focus by Russell Boyd—it deserved a far wider showing than it received from its distributors.

The highlight of the year just had to be the reissue of Columbia's *The Seventh Voyage of Sinbad* in a spruced-up restored print. It was the original 1958 version with *no* cuts, including the entire skeleton duel, the Cyclops roasting a sailor for dinner, and the death of the dragon. The "A" certificate awarded to the movie in 1958 was now reduced to a "U." I couldn't wait to see it and took Stephen along to Redhill's Odeon in September in the hope that the intervening 12 months had forced him to mature a bit since his disastrous visit to *The Golden Voyage of Sinbad*. Fortunately, it had! He sat more or less still in his seat, goggle-eyed throughout the entire picture, and expectedly had bad dreams about the Cyclops for several nights afterwards. Therefore, this made a mockery of one newspaper review of the film which stated solemnly, "Columbia's groundbreaking fantasy was considered too frightening for children when first released in the United Kingdom in 1959, but now Ray Harryhausen's jerky rubber monsters will have little effect on the kids of today." Harryhausen's jerky rubber monsters, however, were still far more scintillating and realistic than those exhibited in one of 1975's new releases. This was *The Land that Time Forgot*, whose paper-mache dinosaurs were encountered by Doug McClure and the crew of a supply ship in 1916. They were on a level with the creatures that menaced Richard Denning and company in 1948's *Unknown Island*—CGI effects were still a long way off!

The 1970s, I concluded one weekend in 1976 with a fellow fantasy film buff, was turning out to be an extremely rum decade indeed as far as HSFF went. This was due to the fact that no set pattern was emerging, there was a general falling-off in excellence, and there was nobody around to replace the directorial skills (in this medium anyway) of Terence Fisher, Jack Arnold, Edward L. Cahn, and others of their ilk. Shoddy special effects abounded that hadn't really progressed since the heady old days of the 1950s. A case in point was the film *At the Earth's Core,* which had its array of odd-looking cardboard-type creatures inhabiting a vast cavern at the center of the globe. They were visited by eccentric scientist Peter Cushing in his Victorian burrowing machine. Violence was the name of the game. Everything seemed much rougher, louder, and somehow imbued with a streak of unpleasantness, which was something the majority of the movies of yesteryear did not possess. However, *they* could be nasty on occasions. Hammer stumbled on with *To the Devil a Daughter*, which was a better-than-average adaptation of the famous Dennis Wheatley black magic book. Its novelty factor was seeing veteran American actor Richard Widmark starring in a British horror movie instead of a Western or detective thriller. He played a writer of the occult and was pitted against the satanic Christopher Lee, who is intent on delivering a spawn of the Devil on mankind. It was a very brief revival in quality for the company before they eventually folded. Steven Spielberg's *Jaws* was a colossal smash and the biggest hit of the decade. Albeit with an enormous plastic shark as the main protagonist, the action was skillfully managed by the director. Although the first half suffered from bouts of pretentious dialogue and the chief villain, when finally revealed, was really no different to the giant creatures seen in countless '50s pictures, despite the fortune spent on constructing it. Having said that, John Williams contributed an instantly recognizable score, which was one of the '70s best by a mile and there were one or two moments of genuine shock to appease the most battle-hardened horror fan.

Critically mauled at the time, but a film that has grown in prestige with age, was *Logan's Run*. Originally, it was to have been a George Pal production, but he was dropped at the last minute by MGM, who carried on with Michael Anderson in the director's seat. In 2274, people inhabiting a boundless domed city are disposed of at the age of 30 to keep the population youthful. Michael York and the delectable Jenny Agutter, who was in a very short tunic, decide to oppose the system and escape from the city. They meet up with wise old sage Peter Ustinov, who lives in a desolate Washington overgrown with weeds and dense vegetation. These scenes were uncannily evocative, realistic, and the best part of a pretty lively sci-fi fantasy that ended in time-honored tradition with the inhabitants of the domed city set free into the great outdoors.

Without doubt, the year's booby prize for the biggest flop by a long chalk went to the Dino De Laurentiis production of RKO's *King Kong*. I took Stephen up to The Casino cinema in London to catch this much-trumpeted remake of the 1933 classic, even though there was a sneaking suspicion at the back of my mind that a movie of the stature of *King Kong* couldn't possibly warrant a revamp—after all, what was the point? *Kong* was one of those timeless cinematic legends that had embedded itself in the human psyche over a period of 43 years. It had a mixture of innovative effects, thrilling action, and rousing music, which made it one of the most enduring pieces of celluloid in the long history of the silver screen. With no Willis O'Brien and Max Steiner at the helm, what sort of chance did it have to win over a whole new generation of cinema-goers? After sitting through it, I summarized not a lot. A half-jokey script, an updated plot to take in topical environmental oil issues, no dinosaurs, a fake-looking giant plastic snake, unsympathetic leads, and a man in a gorilla suit showed scene-by-scene that it was a complete dud. Worst of all was the ill-conceived $2 million

Jessica Lange in the box-office dud, 1976's *King Kong*.

mechanical robotic Kong model that not only bore no resemblance to the guy in the costume, but moved like a mechanical model, fitful and cumbersome. Thank goodness the contraption was only on screen for a few minutes. It must have been a real embarrassment to everyone connected with the making of the movie. The derailment of the subway train sequence wasn't a patch on the original. This proved that O'Brien's animation, four decades on, was hard to beat and one felt no empathy with the giant ape or indeed heroine Jessica Lange when he tumbled to his death from the World Trade Center buildings after being blasted by helicopters. It wasn't beauty that killed the beast in this scenario—it was the de Laurentiis film studios' treatment of a fabled masterpiece that did it.

Only 23 HSFF movies figured in the 138 films I somehow managed to catch on TV, which were mostly low-quality '60s fare. Almost as an afterthought, BBC2 dispensed with, for unknown reasons, their once-yearly horror/fantasy season and stuck on *The Mummy* (1932), *Dr. Jekyll and Mr. Hyde* (1931), and *King Kong* (1933) in meager compensation. This happened to be a blip, though, and the annual horror show continued in 1977, which redressed the balance to keep us buffs happy. From across the Atlantic, Dan Curtis' 1973 *The Norliss Tapes* made an appearance one night on Channel 4, an agreeable made-for-television supernatural drama concocted in the same vein as the celebrated Kolchak TV movies, which were also dreamed up by Curtis (more on that one later). Roy Thinnes played investigative reporter Dan Norliss, who suddenly disappears on an assignment. His editor discovers Norliss' tapes and it transpires throughout the story that the reporter was on the trail of a terminally ill man, who makes a pact with an evil being. Whereby, on the promise of eternal life, he impregnates a clay statue with the blood of a murder victim, thus enabling the ancient devil to enter our world via the statue. Unlike Kolchak, there were no sequels to *The Norliss Tapes*—the feature would have done quite well on the cinema circuits, but Thinnes was no Darren McGavin (the bullish Carl Kolchak) and probably could not have carried a complete series on his own. Nevertheless, it was a neat addition to the American television-horrors that once in a while turned up on our shores. Rather oddly, it hasn't been seen on TV since.

There was no getting away from it. The fantasy scene as a whole was in the doldrums, although the continental horror film was just alive and kicking. Dario Argento's *Suspiria*, regarding a young American student caught up in a witches' coven at a girls' dancing academy, was a genuinely flesh-crawling thriller containing blood-curdling scenes that miraculously escaped the censor's scissors and a thundering and insistent soundtrack by Goblin, which lingered in the mind long after the picture had reached its gory finale. Something special was needed to kickstart the genre into life and to haul it back from the brink of oblivion, even if it meant the direction it would take would be a different type of beast to that of yesteryear. In 12 months time, computerized effects and huge budgets would rejuvenate, to a certain extent, the fantasy film, but before that,

1977 had to be faced, another year when the dubious delights on display were still distinctly below-average. Michael Winner's unappetizing *The Sentinel*, about a young woman trapped in a mansion inhabited by deformed spirits and her boyfriend destined to be the new guardian to what turned out to be the gateway to hell, suffered from the director's predictable bull-headed approach and was none-too-scary, despite the presence of a sterling cast of stalwarts including John Carradine and Eli Wallach. *The People That Time Forgot*, the follow-up to *The Land that Time Forgot*, was endowed with effects even shoddier than many of Bert I. Gordon's '50s efforts. Gordon's own *The Food of the Gods* contained the same old split-screen monstrosities that were a highlight (or should that be lowlight) of *The Amazing Colossal Man*, *The Cyclops* et al. Slightly more satisfying was a trip to the massive Victoria cinema in London to see a rare (in this latter part of the decade) British horror double bill: Hammer's lackluster *Vampire Circus* with Tyburn's *Legend of the Werewolf*, a low-key, but fairly beguiling variation on Hammer's own *The Curse of the Werewolf*. Climbing up the steps between the banks of stalls in the Victoria's cathedral-like auditorium was akin to scaling the side of a mountain. The aisles were steep, which made it quite an event to catch these two moderately watchable outings in such awesome surroundings, even though there were only about 35 people present at the time in a building designed to house at least two thousand customers.

The Omen continued the cinema's current obsession with the Devil and all his works. This was big-scale treatment, super cast, expensive, glossy, but, like *The Exorcist* before it, lacked in nuance, the accent firmly on one gruesome slaying after another to the point of tedium and Damien the Devil-child was far too cute to be menacing. The same could be said for *Audrey Rose*, a heavy-handed indigestible lump of reincarnation nonsense concerning a child killed in a car crash who is reborn into the body of a 12-year-old. Anthony Hopkins attempts to exorcise the spirit of the dead girl, despite skepticism from the girl's parents. Then in September, Harryhausen's latest *Sinbad* incarnation, *Sinbad and the Eye of the Tiger*, appeared in a hard-edged climate of sex and violence, which was a throwback to a distant age. But full marks to the maestro for at least persevering in his endeavors to carry on the tradition of proper fantasy filmmaking against the odds, even if the outcome of his perfected graft lacked narrative drive and the process work, particularly in the final 30 minutes or so, a little obvious by Harryhausen's own high standards. However, notwithstanding these quibbles, and the fact that Patrick Wayne was the limpest Sinbad to date, I enjoyed the flick a lot more than *The Golden Voyage of Sinbad*. In its own rambling and semi-mythical way, it appeared to possess more of a mystical and old-fashioned air to it than *Golden Voyage*. Also, the Troglodyte was one of Harryhausen's most enchanting creations since the euphoric days of *The Seventh Voyage of Sinbad* and *Jason and the Argonauts*, which were undoubtedly his two most highly acclaimed features.

The real oddity of 1977 was *Capricorn One*, an uneasy potpourri of science fiction and James Bond-type action that didn't go down too well with the critics, but, like *Logan's Run*, is another of those slightly undisciplined pictures made during this period, which appears more viewable now than when it was first released. Could a Mars landing be faked to appease presidential self-esteem? That was the premise in Peter Hyams' briskly directed thriller, where three astronauts are forced to play ball with NASA's plans to proceed with a bogus Mars mission. When they are instructed to vacate their life-threatening ship, they realize that, in order to maintain secrecy, their lives will have to be terminated. A laudable cast included Elliott Gould as a scatty  reporter on the trail of the elaborate hoax, an oily Hal Holbrook as the head of NASA command, and Telly Savalas as a mad crop-duster coming to the rescue of beleaguered astronaut James Brolin. Fast-moving and with a cleverly staged trumped-up Mars landing constructed on a stage in a vast hangar, this was a highly enjoyable slice of hokum in the exploitation-mad '70s and all the more refreshing because of its numerous excesses and switches in mood.

Television was at last coming up trumps as BBC2 continued with their annual season of HSFF under the Fantasy-Horror banner, which screened a host of double bills from the '30s and '40s on a Saturday night. It included the entire Universal *Frankenstein* back catalogue (excluding *Abbott and Costello Meet Frankenstein*)—22 movies broadcast over 11 weeks. Again, with no means of taping these programs, crawling into bed at 3:00 a.m. became the norm over this period. It often resulted in headaches for the whole day of Sunday and a complete lack of concern for my sorry state from my partner. In fact, 1977 was a decent year for the British fantasy fan on the box. I sat through 105 films and 38 were HSFF, which was a good return for a change.

1978 was an interesting year in more ways than one. Several old films were re-released in their original 3-D format for what appeared to be a gimmicky reason (as some of the more cynical critics intimated in the press). It was a ploy to obtain more financial mileage out of them and was presented in London at specialized theaters. The fantasy sector was represented by *House of Wax* and a tantalizing double billing of *Creature from the Black Lagoon* and *It Came from Outer Space*. Reclassified "AA," *House of Wax* was shown at The Warner in London's West End. Sitting comfortably in the cinema's palatial auditorium, in a full house, and peering through the infamous green and red plastic lenses housed in their white cardboard frames, Warner Brothers' 1953 garish horror classic looked a treat in three-dimension. For a couple of hours, including adverts and trailers, I was transported back to the golden days between 1962 and 1966 when goodies like this were on offer everywhere and every week of the year.

Universal's two revered fantasy features had also been reclassified. In these more liberal times, *Creature from the Black Lagoon* was now certified an "A" from an "X," while *It Came from Outer Space* was now a "U" from an "A." It was amazing to realize that only 10 years ago, they had been going the rounds with their original certificates. I smiled at the thought. Taking Stephen with me, I had to troop up to London to see the pair at the tiny and rather ornate Eros cinema near Piccadilly Circus. Queuing up to buy our tickets, we were each handed the special glasses and had made our way into the cramped auditorium. It was almost full by mostly older patrons, who had no doubt watched these two movies years ago in normal flat screen and were intrigued as to what they would look like in 3-D. The lights dimmed, the curtains rolled back, and like my visit to *House of Wax*, I was carried along on a wave of nostalgia to the dazzling and halcyon days of the 1960s. As *It Came from Outer Space* commenced, the stereoscopic effects were not really all that impressive, but matters were not helped by a relatively small screen. Ten minutes into the picture, Stephen nudged me in the gloom.

"Dad. I can't see through these glasses."

I squinted at him. "Why? What's wrong with them?"

"Don't know," he whispered. "It looks all green and funny."

I peered at Stephen again. In the flickering light, I could just about make out the problem—my son's glasses were on the wrong way round! I whisked them off, bent the frames back in reverse, and stuck them back on the correct way.

"Any better?"

He stared fixedly at the screen. "Yes thanks."

Curious, I took mine off and put them on with the red and green lenses swapped over. The movie did have, as Stephen had correctly stated, a greenish hue about it and the 3-D was nowhere in evidence. I put them back on correctly in case eye strain took over, which in my case, normally gave me one hell of a headache and concentrated on the rest of Jack Arnold's seminal sci-fi picture. Though, I must admit, it was not as forceful a film as the monster thrillers he knocked out for Universal afterwards, it was still streets ahead in artistic content to what passed as science fiction in the 1970s.

Creature from the Black Lagoon's effects were much more arresting and had made Stephen jump a few times, especially when Hans J. Salter's full-blooded score kicked in. Blimey, I thought, 11 years ago in 1967, I had watched the gill-man flick when it was an "X" on a double bill with Lugosi's *Dracula*, which also sported Britain's infamous restrictive adult rating. Now my eight-year-old son was sitting next to me taking it all in. What a funny old world it was. Still, it almost brought a tear to my eye being subjected to a couple of 1950s black-and-white sci-fi/horror movies, even though, when emerging into the glare of the late August sunshine, they seemed a bit of an anachronism. For they were surrounded by gaudy billboards that advertised a nearby James Bond double bill: *Live and Let Die* and *The Man With the Golden Gun* along with *One Flew Over the Cuckoo's Nest* and *McArthur–The Rebel General*. Universal's last-ditch double fantasy bill belonged to another time and place, not London in 1978.

Warlords of Atlantis, the latest addition in the series of Kevin Connor and John Dark fantasy adventures, reworked the old lost city of Atlantis myth. The special effects were an improvement on their previous efforts (*The Land that Time Forgot*, *The People that Time Forgot* and *At the Earth's Core*), but it was still fantasy fodder for children. With square-jawed hero Doug McClure freeing slaves from the tyranny of mad ruler Daniel Massey and having to cope with some way-out monsters in the process, it was corny, but fun all the same.

Like a throwback to the double bills of the 1950s and 1960s came a pairing of "AA" features, *The Savage Bees* and *The Incredible Melting Man*. The first was a hoary grade Z thriller originally made for American television, but given a cinema release in Britain. It was about a swarm of African killer bees that, having decimated large areas of South America, create havoc in New Orleans during the Mardi Gras festival. A pretty dumb excuse for a horror flick, *The Savage Bees* only added to the old adage that bees do not, by any stretch of the imagination, make good movie monsters. The second part of this double billing was a hybrid mix of both *The Quatermass Experiment* and *First Man into*

Space and was vastly inferior to both of them in every conceivable department. After picking up an infection in space, an astronaut returns from Saturn and turns into a flesh-eating ghoul. Cue for the monster to go lurching around like an overgrown gooey mess and frightening people, but not the audience! This turned out to be a fine example of how not to make a decent sci-fi/horror film. Director William Sachs should have concentrated more on the product of the 1950s to see how it ought to have been done because, from a cinematic point of view, that particular decade may have had its faults, but producing fare like *The Incredible Melting Man* wasn't one of them. Pictures such as these had been made with great expertise, year in and year out, and even the worst of the bunch used to have one or two strong points to recommend it. Sachs' pastiche, if that was what the intention was, didn't have any.

At the beginning of the year, the latest smash hit from across the water, *Star Wars*, opened in London to the decade's biggest load of ballyhoo and a colossal fanfare of hype. It heralded state-of-the-art computerized special effects and a new high in realism (claimed the blurbs and the producers) not seen since *2001: A Space Odyssey*. However, the chief difference between these two sci-fi epics was that Kubrick's masterwork appealed to the more cerebral clientele (myself included!), whereas George Lucas's space fairy tale, which blatantly plundered scenes and dialogue from countless other films including *Metropolis* and even *The Dam Busters* (look at the climax again—you'll see what I mean), was without a shadow of a doubt aimed unequivocally at the juvenile end of the market. More importantly, it marked the beginning of mass merchandising within the cinema industry, with everything on sale relating to the film, from models of the *Millennium Falcon,* to stormtrooper's helmets. It was a gigantic money spinning machine, all merchandise for the kids to spend their new-found wealth on. Adults were left firmly and squarely behind. Yes, a major science fiction/fantasy movie was responsible for all of this and *Star Wars* has a lot to answer for. After forking out a fiver to view it in London, I remained unimpressed by the cartoon-style horseplay present in *Star Wars*, whether it was coining in the millions or not. In my lofty opinion, it was all flash, bang, wallop, and no substance. Harrison Ford should have been the main lead and not the wimpy Mark Hamil. Quite often, the picture appeared to be wallowing in its own self-indulgence, as if smugly patting itself on the back for being so damned clever. *Forbidden Planet* and *This Island Earth* did it so much better, even on smaller budgets and without the aid of computers. On the plus side, the opening shot of Hamill's ship being pursued by a giant battle cruiser through a vast inky space over Tatooine was simply jaw-dropping. The *Falcon*'s navigator and big hairy Chewbacca were an engaging addition to sci-fi's hall of space creatures. Darth Vader made a passable villain and John Williams contributed a fine score, which unfortunately was overused in the follow-ups. Granted a "U" certificate for general release, the film lacked the necessary gritty edge

Harrison Ford and Mark Hamil try to save Princess Leia in *Star Wars*.

and more importantly, for a film of this type, a sense of wonder, while the two robots, R2-D2 and C-3PO, were amusing for the first 25 minutes before their Laurel and Hardy-type tomfoolery began to pall. One U.K. critic called it "a multimillion-dollar empty bag of tricks" and another labeled it "heroes and villains in space." Perhaps the two were devotees of the '50s style of science fiction because I couldn't have put it better myself.

Spielberg's *Close Encounters of the Third Kind* kept the momentum rolling with this brand-new cycle of overblown and effects-laden science fiction movies, 135 very long minutes that started promisingly enough, fell flat in the middle and perked up towards the grand finale when the alien's mother ship communicated with both the scientists and a bemused Richard Dreyfuss. A major irritation was the director's preoccupation with lighting, which was a trademark of most of his work, but done to death in this one. With shafts and beams of light appearing from behind doors, windows, curtains, and the various UFOs, there was a certain amount of "what a smart chap I am" about the whole shebang. It may have been good to look at, but I emerged from the Odeon in Croydon a tad frustrated by Spielberg's clodhopping and rather hollow sci-fi extravaganza. I was still yearning for days gone by when the product on display zipped along for 85 minutes instead of two hours plus. Unfortunately, the five notes used by the scientists to relay messages to the aliens were still buzzing infuriatingly in my head.

The other inflated and over-promoted fantasy motion picture of 1978 was *Superman the Movie*, a big-budgeted revamp of the old Marvel comics' hero that dragged its heels over 142 minutes, where the effects were a bit hit and miss. The opening sequence was set on Krypton with Marlon Brando, pantomime-like in its staginess and the normally reliable Gene Hackman overacting like a man possessed as the chief villain, Lex Luthor. Christopher Reeve shone as Superman himself, fitted that costume and those tights nicely, but the movie seemed to me to be a disorganized series of episodes that didn't gel. It was not the sum total of its parts and although a big financial success, I studiously ignored the two follow-ups that appeared in 1980 and 1983.

I sat through 97 movies on television that year, where a measly 25 were fantasy and 16 were figured in BBC2's Horror Double Bill, which broadcast in July and commenced at midnight. To give some idea of how these double bills were thrown together and to show their appeal value to the genre connoisseur, I list the full complement below:

The Murders in the Rue Morgue (1932) and *The Man Who Could Cheat Death* (1959)
The Fantastic Disappearing Man (1957) and *The Man with X-Ray Eyes* (1963)
The Quatermass Experiment (1955) and *Gorgo* (1961)
The Mummy's Curse (1944) and *House of Wax* (1953)
The Incredible Shrinking Man (1957) and *Phantom of the Rue Morgue* (1953)
The Curse of Frankenstein (1957) and *The Mummy's Shroud* (1966)
Vampire Circus (1971) and *The Pit and the Pendulum* (1961)
The Vampire Lovers (1970) and *The Lost Continent* (1968)

You will agree that this is a fine selection. Therefore, it is all the more galling to conclude that today's British terrestrial TV listings (as opposed to satellite television, but this is no better in this respect) are devoid of program material such as the cycle of HSFF movies that BBC2 ran in the '70s and part of the 1980s.

At last, the BBC screened *Journey to the Center of the Earth* in its complete length (no cuts thank goodness) and this more than made up for the lack of HSFF fodder on the box. An unscathed print of *King Kong* was also shown on the BBC They were in favor of showing any film in its original form, not saddled by time restrictions and advertisements as on the commercial channels, which still persisted in slicing up movies to squeeze into the time slots and was a constant source of annoyance among us movie buffs.

The decade ended on an upbeat note with the release of Ridley Scott's *Alien*—finally, an "X" certificate adult sci-fi/horror movie set in space with tremendous special effects, a believable cast, expert direction, a haunting score, and (although not seen for most of the picture) one of the most original and eye-catching demons in sci-fi history courtesy of designer H.R. Giger. Before *Alien* literally burst onto Britain's cinema circuits, the first of three second-class remakes hit the screen at the beginning of the year. *Invasion of the Body Snatchers*, a gruesome rehash of the Siegel 1956 classic that wasn't too bad by '70s standards, but lacked the paranoia and urgency of the original, and it had a nice touch to feature the original's Kevin McCarthy in a small cameo role. *Nosferatu the Vampyre* was shown in a few of London's art-house cinemas and was deemed a little too continental for general release, so I took it in at The Curzon in Mayfair. A careful, almost scholarly, reworking of the landmark 1922 F.W. Murnau production with Klaus Kinski, who turned in an eerily effective performance as the loathsome bloodsucker, was spooky, but not paced enough for a mass audience. It relied more on brooding and cobwebby atmospherics than bloody mayhem and everything better for it.

Meanwhile, Universal resurrected *Dracula* in a new up market guise. Frank Langella, who played the fangless vampire count, was pitted against Laurence Olivier's Van Helsing. The film was lush and expensive, but in the eyes of many horror fans it was a failure. Langella was more like a 1930s matinee idol than a vampire, the confrontations between the two protagonists were weakly portrayed (Christopher Lee and Peter Cushing's spats remain the benchmark), and the climax, whereby Dracula was hoisted up a ship's mast into the sunlight, was badly executed. Notwithstanding, the ghoulish female vampire victims, who were distinctly not scary in spite of the "X" rating, this was a disappointing entry in cinema's long love affair with the undead. Far more worthwhile, but lower in tone, was George A. Romero's *Martin*, a modernistic vampire tale in which one is left to decide whether or not the blood-drinking youth of the title is a vampire or simply a serial killer. Cheaply made in handheld camera mode, it at least gave a different slant to

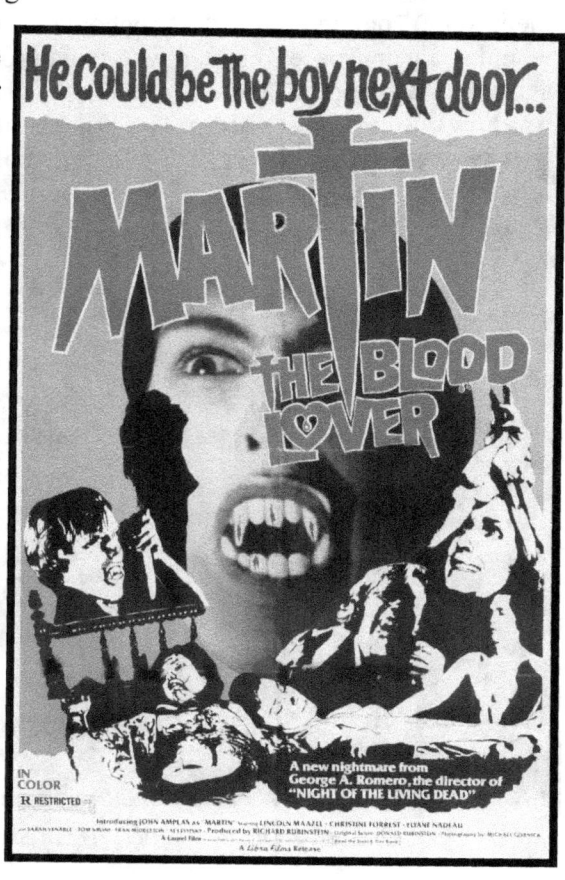

39

the old legend, but the movie did not make it onto the major circuits, for it was considered to be too arty for a provincial release. I traveled up to London to catch it at a very restrictive and poky cinema off Leicester Square. Large cinemas were on the way out (but would return with a vengeance 10 years later). Smaller and elegantly furnished venues were now fashionable and appealed to those requiring a cozy and intimate atmosphere in which to view a film. They contained two or three screens in one theater, where each plushy carpeted auditorium sat around 100 people. *Martin* was projected onto the tiniest screen I had ever come across. It was a rectangle no bigger than what many television screens would become in the home cinema boom of the late 1990s. The tinny sound emanating from the auditorium's sound system was, to put it bluntly, manifestly low-fi. As I paid a whopping (it was back then!) £6.00 to sit through it, plus train fare, I felt short-changed by the whole experience—it was never like this at the Odeon in Epsom in 1962!

But, as previously mentioned, the year's key fantasy release had to be *Alien*, an expensive retake of *It! The Terror from Beyond Space*. The film was one of the few science fiction movies to accurately (or as accurate as one could imagine it to be) conjure up the claustrophobic terror suffered by a crew of seven manning a giant space freighter, who fought for their lives in confined spaces against an unstoppable foe. "A superior haunted house chiller set in space" was how one critic described it. The striking biomechanical imagery conjured

Our first glimpse of the new *Enterprise* in *Star Trek: The Motion Picture*.

up by designer H.R. Giger was a huge influence for every major sci-fi picture that was to follow. Too slow-burning for some, the chest-bursting sequence had the audience I was seated with screaming in revulsion. My only quibble concerning the film was that Giger's adult alien was not allowed a great deal of screen time. It's a pity considering the amount of time, effort, and money the man had spent in creating the thing. A little less restraint would have worked wonders, but the way in which Scott racked up the tension, the cast, the unique production design (particularly the abandoned alien vessel on the planetoid) was top-notch. The picture was definitely light years ahead of 1979's other much-lauded release: *Star Trek: The Motion Picture,* the cinema version of television's hugely popular *Star Trek.*

Paramount's sci-fi spectacular was, it has to be said, a monumental bore, even with noted director Robert Wise at the helm. I, along with countless Trekkie nuts, was an avid fan of the exalted TV series. Although it was a treat to see those iconic and well-loved characters on the giant Panavision screen (the Starship Enterprise was magnificent as well), they looked a lot older and the movie took an age to get into gear. There was too much reverential screen-time spent in introducing Kirk, Spock, Bones, Scotty, and the rest of the cast as if they were Greek gods who had just stepped down from Mount Olympus instead of a ship's crew. We all know who they are, I sighed, fidgeting in my seat, just get on with it. And when they did get on with it, the result was a let-down, a bum-numbing never-ending journey to discover the origin of a strange force that was destroying everything in its path and heading towards Earth, only to find that the object was an old voyager space probe returning home, programmed by an alien race to gather information and bent on destroying the planet because no one had responded to its signals. The mind-boggling visuals apart (courtesy of Douglas Trumbull), *Star Trek: The Motion Picture* came across as uninspiring and ponderous. The picture made a fortune as expected, but that didn't necessarily mean it was an advancement on the television series, which despite (or because of) its wobbly effects, camp plots, and attention to the quirkiness of the characters, retained an endearing quality that the movie simply did not possess.

Almost on the same level as *Star Trek: The Motion Picture* in terms of creakiness was *Meteor*, a disaster of a disaster movie, whereby a notable cast including Natalie Wood and Sean 'James Bond' Connery were among a group of scientists awaiting the destruction of Earth by a giant asteroid. Fragments of it were causing all kinds of catastrophes to occur. A banal script, some appalling special effects, stereotyped characters, and garish color photography put this picture firmly in the bargain-basement bracket—it was done a whole lot more convincingly in some of the '50s minor efforts and with a fraction of the cost as well.

BBC2 continued their annual fantasy season under the new heading of "Masters of Terror," giving Warner Brothers' *Doctor X* its television premier in a primitive color print, but only 25 HSFF movies were included in the 83 I saw on the small screen that year, many of which were oft-repeated—*Psycho, Dracula Has Risen from the Grave, The Hound of the Baskervilles* (1959), and *It Came from Outer Space* had all been on before and more than once. Nothing new or different was being broadcast. No '30s or '40s classics and no '50s B features. Where on earth were they all? I often wondered, as I gave up on the umpteenth showing of *The Devil Rides Out* and retired for the night, not daring to risk another headache to add to all the others I had endured in the name of fantasy, sitting glued to these old horror movies at 1:30 in the morning when all sane people should have been fast asleep between the sheets.

To atone somewhat for the paucity of HSFF on television, ITV presented towards the end of the year a brand-new *Quatermass* serial entitled quite simply *Quatermass* or *Quatermass IV*. Nigel Kneale had originally offered the screenplay to the BBC nine years previously, but the British Broadcasting Corporation, responsible for scaring the living daylights out of the viewing public with the first three *Quatermass* serials in the 1950s, had, for reasons of their own, not taken up the option. Veteran English actor John Mills was brought in to play the Professor, who suspects that an alien force, who wiped out a joint American-Russian space mission, is responsible for harvesting whole groups of hippie-type youngsters, the Planet People, who wish to escape from an England that has descended into anarchy, believing that they are being beamed up to a better world than the one they inhabit. The alien presence is finally destroyed by tricking it into homing in on a nuclear device, which is detonated by the Professor's assistant, for Quatermass had succumbed to a fatal heart attack. *Quatermass* was broadcast in four one-hour episodes and repeated in 1984, a 105-minute version under the title of *The Quatermass Conclusion* cobbled together for an abortive theatrical release, which didn't go down too well with Nigel Kneale. Although interestingly enough as a piece of television fantasy drama, *Quatermass* failed to match up to the incredible impact of its predecessors: *The Quatermass Experiment, Quatermass 2,* and *Quatermass and the Pit*, all of which had held the whole of Great Britain in their thrall by causing viewers to hide behind their sofas and not venture out on dark nights! John Mills was fine in the title role, but the documentary-type intensity that was a hallmark of the infamous *Quatermass* '50s trilogy was no longer there—like the 1970s brand of cinema sci-fi/fantasy, the latest reincarnation of Kneale's favorite character was a shadow of its former self. (Note: After many years of waiting, *The Quatermass Experiment* (1953), *Quatermass 2* (1955), and *Quatermass and the Pit* (1958/1959) are now available on DVD. Regrettably, only the first two episodes of *Experiment* have survived, but even those have an eerie quality about them. Haunting images that echo down the decades, a reminder to buffs of the innovative nature of these primitive [by today's standards] and groundbreaking science fiction television melodramas.)

John Carpenter's highly popular *Halloween* double billed with a movie that ran into more censorship problems in some parts of the United Kingdom: *House of Whipcord*. *Halloween* heralded the commencement of the teen-slasher school of horror cinema with a bang and rounded off the decade nicely. It was a Hitchcock-style updating of the old "bogeyman will get you" scenario as a masked killer stalks his prey in a small town on Halloween night—I then, one evening, took stock with a fellow enthusiast, Neil, over a pint of beer in our local pub.

"Well, what do you think of all this '70s stuff then?"

"Crap."

He was only confirming my own thoughts on the subject, but I pressed on. "Yeah, well OK, let's expand on that."

"Listen, Baz, I don't have to expand on it all that much. You were around in the good old days and I caught the tail end of it. Those good old days are well and truly finished, mate."

"Reckon so?"

"Know so. No Hammer. No double bills—well, the odd one or two maybe, but not like they used to be. No late-nighters. No decent horror. And sci-fi—blimey. *Star Wars*, *Close Encounters,* and *Star Trek*. You don't honestly like them, do you?"

"Not a lot. Trouble is most these new films are U-rated so they lack, er… what's the word?"

"Balls?"

"Yeah. Balls. Spot on. The old stuff, you know, the old *Frankenstein* and *Dracula* flicks, the Hammers, *Tarantula*, *Creature from the Black Lagoon*, all those dozens, no *hundreds*, of flicks I saw in the '60s, well, they were darker, more gutsy, more forceful, shorter, more *oomph*. Good build-up, which didn't take too long, then straight into the action, no messing around. Great actors as well, you know, the old school of acting, most of them ex-stage—Karloff,

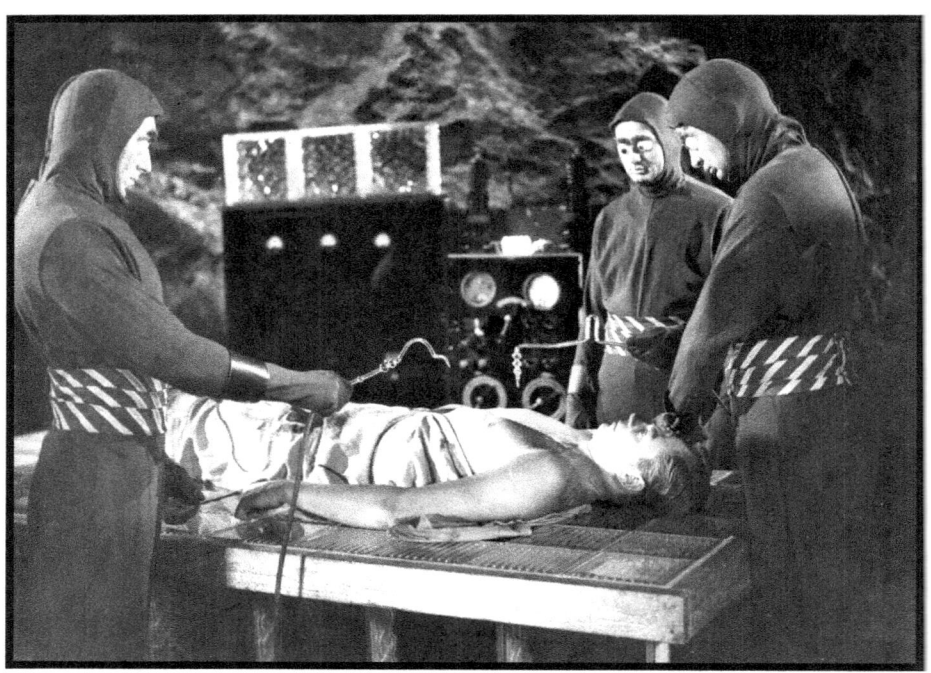

You just don't get the quality stuff like *Killers from Space* anymore!

Lugosi, Zucco, John Agar, Denning, Thompson, Lee, Cushing, Price. Where are they all today? Tell me that."

"And let us not forget that the majority of the oldies were 'X' films."

"Yeah, that's the crux of the matter. Everything's for the bloody kids nowadays. I don't know—there's no style to any of it, the color is horrible, and as for the music."

"Ah! I thought you'd get onto that subject."

"Bloody right I am. It's too loud, too harsh, and absolutely lacking in melody. Think about it. All the great horror soundtracks come from the '30s, '40s and '50s."

"What about the 1960s?"

"I honestly believe that's when it all went wrong. Somewhere along the line, the two and a half to three-minute burst of music, over the opening credits that somehow had to summarize the entire mood of the picture you were about to be subjected to, has been abandoned. OK, fair dos, the music in *Star Wars* isn't too bad, but it does go on a bit and that's the trouble—it's too grandiose, too full of itself."

"Like the pictures themselves?"

"Yes, exactly. Widescreen, millions of dollars, long running times, dull photography, flashy direction, drippy heroes, silly scripts, stereophonic sound at full blast. Break-neck tempo as well. I keep saying to myself, slow down for heaven's sake, what's the bloody rush, let's have a little bit of care and attention here, some atmosphere, some meaningful exchanges in dialogue. I don't know about you, but I used to really adore even chronic stuff like *Killers from Space* and *She Demons* years ago, but none of this modern fodder has much of an effect on me. What about you, do you feel the same?"

"Yes I do, mate. They're boring."

"Oh yeah, another thing. Have you noticed that everybody shouts in films these days?"

"Well, the reason for that is that there's so much racket going on around them, they've got to make themselves heard."

"Maybe that's it. What it all means is that today's batch of movie-makers direct everything at the speed of an express train with no time for anything else and that includes character development, by the way. Surely you've twigged that characters in the latest films, well, you never get to know about them, do you. They're just puppets at the mercy of the backers, mouthing inane dialogue, you can't relate to any of 'em. Wooden is the term I would use."

"Now you're getting technical."

"Well, I'm no expert in these matters, but personally, as the song goes, things aren't what they used to be. From the fantasy genre point of view, I don't think there's the talent around at the moment, who are in tune with their roots, and, let's face it, Spielberg himself has stated in interviews that he was a big fan of stuff like *Creature from the Black Lagoon* when he was a kid—in fact, a lot of today's directors grew up on the old horror movies, in the States anyway. They were a big influence on them. So it's funny the way things are turning out. Go on, admit it, wouldn't it be just great to pop down to the Odeon tonight to see, say, *The Black Scorpion* and *Frankenstein 1970*. You know, relive the old times, just for a few hours. What a treat that would be."

"It would, Baz, but it's not going to happen. I agree with everything you say, but there's no point in getting bitter and twisted over it. Your loyalty to the old classics knows no bounds and is highly commendable! Mind you, *Alien* was great though, wasn't it? And *that* was a '70s flick."

"Yeah, I agree. It was."

"Tell you what—have another drink, it'll make you feel much better."

"Yes, OK. Your round, though."

To summarize that conversation, the 1970s had not really come up with anything to grab my imagination, apart from one or two features (it remains my least-favorite decade for cinema viewing). The total number of films, including HSFF, seen at the cinema between 1971 and 1979 was nowhere near, for instance, the 125 I had sat through in a single year, 1962. The excitement and sheer pleasure ingredients had faded away—the larger cinemas were closing down (Reigate's Hippodrome was one example) or undergoing conversions into nightclubs (as with Redhill's Odeon). Programs now consisted for the most part of

one film only and when that film was over, it was lights on and one had to exit the cinema to make way for the next showing. No staying put in the darkness to sit through all three performances either—those days were over and done with. Special effects in sci-fi movies had admittedly risen to a new level of authenticity, but the You are Watching a Very Important Movie syndrome (present in *Star Wars* and *Star Trek: The Motion Picture*) was a regular pain in the backside to this viewer, who had been brought up on a diet of cheapos, where all concerned had rolled up their sleeves and dirtied their hands to get their pet projects onto the silver screen, despite budget constraints. Pomposity ruled—not a very attractive trait, be it cinema or any other medium. Everything seemed to be drowning in a sea of self-satisfaction. Even Hammer's output had dried up, the company now virtually defunct as far as the cinema was concerned, a sad state of affairs. Surely the 1980s wouldn't carry on with this trend. Is it too much to ask, I said to myself, if the genre got down to the bare basics again, reducing over-long running times and perhaps coming up with the occasional black-and-white feature? Funny enough, while plowing ahead with the multimillion-dollar effects-driven merchandise audiences now demanded, which *did* rake in the money, a few minor treasures did emerge. During the ensuing years, they restored my faith in all things fantastic and prevented me from turning my back on all modern-day fare for good, which at one point, I seriously considered doing.

3
1980-1989

Proving that old habits die hard and harking back to the early part of 1967, when I caught *King Kong* and *The Thing from Another World* five times in two weeks, I saw the X-rated *Alien* a further three times in 1980, once, on a double bill with John Carpenter's *The Fog*, rated "AA," a rarity in itself. Horror double bills were very thin on the ground in 1980 and a packed house at the Odeon in Croydon showed yet again that these kinds of presentations, given the right quality of the movies on offer, could still pull in the punters, as they once did years ago.

In fact, 1980 was a pretty good year, the most rewarding in a long while, and I fervently believed that matters were on the up. Not only were there some acceptable releases out on the circuits, but television screened an unprecedented 35 fantasy films out of 81 seen. BBC2 still carried on with their once-yearly parade of HSFF under the title of "Horror Double Bill," a haphazardly put-together collection ranging from Hammer (*Nightmare*), classics (*The Mad Ghoul*), to old tat (*The Bat*). However, my days of sitting through these, while hopelessly attempting to stay awake until the early hours of the morning, with eyes hurting, head pounding, a nauseous lump in my insides, and waiting for the final credits to roll before I lurched off to bed at 3:00 a.m., were more or less at an end. The video recorder was beginning to make an impact in the U.K. leisure market and was now on offer to the public at an affordable price. So I spent money for a not-too-expensive model, connected it up to the TV, and taped these midnight attractions to enable me to view them at a more reasonable hour instead of the dead of night. This also meant that because of this magical change in my viewing techniques, my movie projector and screen, which was bought in Hong Kong in 1966, and my collection of 50-foot, 200-foot, and 400-foot reels of 8mm film, were consigned to the attic, along with dozens of copies of *Famous Monsters of Filmland*, *Castle of Frankenstein,* and *Mad Monsters* magazines. Most of these little strips of celluloid (purchased in the States in 1965 and 1966) were in a poor state of preservation anyway, with numerous joins where they had snapped in the projection gate, and of course they were silent. Nevertheless, I felt a real pang when I packed them away—at least it *was* celluloid, albeit on a miniature scale. Magnetic tape simply didn't carry the same ambience—it was too impersonal, ugly looking, bulky to store, and it deteriorated more rapidly than film through everyday usage. I never cared much for VHS as a recording medium, but it would be a very long time indeed before something better came along to replace it—DVD.

As stated, the future seemed brighter cinema-wise, but as it turned out, this was destined, for various reasons, not to last. The sequel to the phenomenally successful (but vapid) *Star Wars* appeared in a blaze of publicity, *The Empire Strikes Back*, and was a marked improvement on the first one, I thought. Harrison Ford, as roguish Han Solo, was given a more prominent role, the movie had good pace, and a sharper edge to it. It ditched the sentimentality of its predecessor and looked dazzling as well. Even the comical high jinks of the two droids were toned down and replaced by the wisdom of the Muppet-like Yoda, who, in a somewhat lengthy sequence, teaches Luke Skywalker the secrets of the Force. The special edition of *Close Encounters of the Third Kind* proved that judicious editing with a tagged-on ending could work. For the movie benefitted from Spielberg's (not the censor's) scissors, the flow quickened, the monotonous middle section was trimmed, and a more spectacular climax was created as Richard Dreyfuss and a select group of scientists boarded the mother ship, embarking on a journey into the unknown. *Time After Time* was an inspired mix of H.G. Wells and Jack the Ripper with a fine pairing of David Warner as the Ripper and Malcolm McDowell as Wells, who was on the trail of the serial killer in 1980s San Francisco. It was an underrated picture with a distinctive score, which proved to be an unexpected success in England. Top of the pile was David Lynch's *The Elephant Man*, which was lovingly photographed in grainy black and white to capture the grime of Victorian England. Featuring a tremendously moving performance by John Hurt as the grotesquely deformed John Merrick, who was rescued from an agonizing life of squalor and destitution as a sideshow attraction by kindly surgeon Anthony Hopkins, Lynch's semi-masterpiece was a rarity in this slam-bang aggressive chapter in the cinema's history. It was a beautifully crafted *Freaks*-type picture that both horrified in the heartless treatment meted out to Merrick and tugged at the heartstrings in the closing 10 minutes.

Naturally, there were a couple of bummers doing the rounds. Brian de Palma's *Dressed to Kill* was a lurid cross-dressing psycho-thriller that experienced censorship problems in England because of its graphic murder scenes—Hitchcock would probably have made a more competent job of it. Even worse, or at least a major disappointment, was Kubrick's *The Shining*. To me, Stephen King's novel is one of the greatest haunted house tomes ever written, its subject of a man descending into madness secondary only to the creepy comings and goings-on in the remote Overlook Hotel. Kubrick took the core of the novel's theme, but chose instead to concentrate on Jack Nicholson's inexorable mental deterioration from a family man in charge of the hotel during the winter months to a madman possessed by the hotel's evil spirits. An over-the-top performance as befits this particular actor, but one that detracted from the hotel itself—the movie (which admittedly looked great) wasn't all that spine-chilling and should have conveyed far more of the hotel's ingrained malevolence and powerful ghostly force, which it patently failed to carry off. Shorn of 20 minutes for its British release, I walked out of Reigate's Majestic cinema distinctly underwhelmed.

A director with the clout of Kubrick, I reckoned, could have come up with something more in keeping with King's supernatural vision and at least tried to scare the pants off people instead of boring them.

Saturn 3 nearly entered the bummer category, but not quite. Lambasted by the critics, this ragbag sci-fi brew about an eight-foot robot on a space station lusting after Farrah Fawcett, herself protected by an aging Kirk Douglas, was apparently beset by production problems after set designer John Barry died midway through the picture. Harvey Keitel, as the robot's demented creator, turned in the only credible performance—as the running time was a miserable 87 minutes, one felt that somewhere along the line, the best of the action had ended up on the cutting room floor as the movie had an undeniably disjointed feel to it.

1981 continued the upward trend at a pace, commencing with Spielberg's *Raiders of the Lost Ark*, a rattling salute to the old serials of the 1930s and 1940s with a superb spectral climax whereby the Ark of the Covenant is opened by the evil Nazis, which unleashes a horde of wraith-like demons bent on vengeance. It was probably this one scene that earned the movie an "A" certificate. Cronenberg's repellent *The Brood* and the equally gory *Scanners* (gaining notoriety because of its exploding head scene) went the rounds as a double "X" bill, as did *The Funhouse* and *My Bloody Valentine*, being two adult-orientated teen shockers that really did deliver the goods in thrills and suspense. Another off-the-wall double program, which continued this unexpected run of back-to-back presentations, was Ken Russell's *Altered States* teamed up with *It Lives Again*. In Russell's weird and occasionally wonderful take on the Jekyll-Hyde fable, William Hurt was the man who, through submersion in a sensory deprivation tank, regressed into a primitive ape-like life form and committed a string of murders when in his regressed state. The bombardment of psychedelic images towards the end as Hurt overdoses on regression, mutating from one monstrous being to another, became wearisome, although this was typical of Russell in his prime. But at least the movie steered clear of the rest of the pack, as did Larry Cohen's sequel to *It's Alive*, which featured not one, but several of the mutant, bug-eyed, and fanged babies scuttling around in the shadows, causing all kinds of mischief. Not a great success as a double bill at the time, both movies have unaccountably failed to turn up on television over the intervening years.

The Howling, a semi-spoof on Universal's golden age of horror movies (all the characters were named after the personnel who were involved in those vintage oldies) contained man-into-werewolf transformation scenes that were unnervingly and terrifyingly real, and *Alien* was still out on the circuits. Ridley Scott's space chiller proved to be a durable hit at the box office and no wonder—buffs knew a good thing when they saw it and *Alien* was definitely a classic in the making, if classics existed at all in the 1980s.

I was expecting another dose of *Howling*-type mayhem when I went along to Croydon's Odeon to catch the X-rated *Wolfen,* but left feeling bitterly dissatisfied considering the effort I had made to travel up to Croydon to see it, not to mention the high cost of the ticket and the train fare. Werewolves were in short

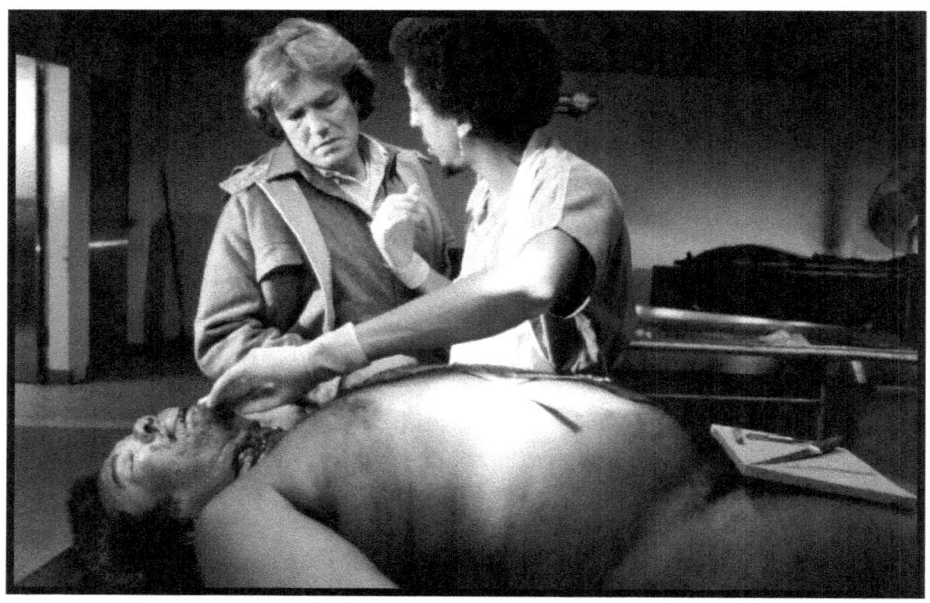

Albert Finney and Gregory Hines managed to find one werewolf in *Wolfen*.

supply in this movie—in fact they were non-existent! Britain's Albert Finney played a New York detective investigating a number of savage killings, only to discover that they were being carried out by a pack of oversized wolves: The Wolfen of the title, who were the original denizens of the city and had existed side-by-side with man, while remaining undetected. The feeble ending had Finney and his Indian assistant surrounded by the wolves, almost on the verge of communicating with them by telepathy. Finney's performance aside, *Wolfen* was a murder mystery masquerading as an implausible horror thriller, a combination that, in this instance, failed to set the box office alight and managed to hoodwink the paying customers into the bargain by leading them to believe that they were going to see something that didn't manifest itself onto the big screen.

In April, a perennial favorite of mine turned up out of the blue for a one-off Saturday morning showing at Reigate's Majestic cinema, *Jason and the Argonauts*. Needless to say, I quickly ran hot-footed to the cinema, with Stephen and my seven-year-old daughter Tracy, to catch the movie, sitting through the excruciating *The 12 Tasks of Asterix* before Bernard Herrmann's pounding title theme announced the start to one of Ray Harryhausen's most noteworthy flights of fancy, a marvelous slice of Greek mythology that put most present-day fare of its sort very firmly in the shade. The auditorium was full, mostly with kids, and my two lapped it up. Also, the print was in fine fettle for an 18-year-old picture, the Dynamation imagery was just as magical as it had always been, and as for that memorable music—it sent tingles of pleasure up my spine, making me conscious of the fact that scores such as this one were without question a thing of the past. From one of the maestro's finest, the three of us attended Harryhausen's last-ever production in July, *Clash of the Titans*. By now, the man himself, in the closing stages of his career, must have been fully aware that his singular type of fantasy did not fit in well with a 1980s audience, who were fast becoming used to more elaborate, but far blander, computerized effects. He had decided to call it a day with this swansong, which was a pity. For his vivid and three-dimensional models were heaps more arresting than the computer generated figures seen in, say, *Star Wars, The Empire Strikes Back,* and the spate of dinosaur movies that were to snowball over the oncoming years. But whereas the newer fantasy movies had, in many cases, over 100 technicians working to create what came up on the big screen, Harryhausen, like Willis O'Brien before him, was in sole charge of his effects, a one-man band, beavering away for months on end in the studios just to piece together a five-minute sequence, but the kind of sequence us aficionados had come to appreciate over the years. The great man must have become disillusioned after spending the best part of a year on his pictures only to see them scoffed at by the snooty, unappreciative critics. *Clash of the Titans* was a mite too dark and heavy-going for the youngsters, hence the "A" certificate, and had a seen it all before air about it (the picture was mostly panned by the press), but the movie did contain one of the master's greatest moments: Perseus's confrontation with the Gorgon, Medusa, on the Isle of the Dead, a unique combination of stop-motion animation, suspense, and even horror that was a fitting tribute to one of fantasy cinema's most celebrated practitioners of this specific and highly specialized art-form.

Both the late-night shows and the Sunday one-day attractions were now a part of local cinema folklore. However, for a short while only during the early '80s, a slightly offbeat and rather unorthodox method of screening feature films came along to pander to those of us who required not only at least two attractions for the price of a ticket, but something a little more unfamiliar in the way of program presentations—the multi-program. Four to five movies were shown one after the other with no adverts (thankfully) and no trailers. They often commenced in the early afternoon and finished (which allowed for several refreshment breaks) around seven to eight hours later. The films stuck on were all themed—to illustrate this, in 1978 I had caught the train to Croydon, where a small independent two-in-one cinema was presenting, on a Sunday afternoon, all four Beatles' classics (*A Hard Day's Night, Help!, Yellow Submarine,* and *Let It Be*) together with Gerry and the Pacemakers' *Ferry Cross the Mersey*. The adjacent auditorium was screening five Elvis Presley vehicles in contrast with Presley fans wandering into the Merseybeat program by mistake and vice versa, which lead to bouts of shouting and swearing! I had also managed, without too much fuss and bother, to sit through a marathon nine-hour session at The Majestic in Reigate when the fodder on display was Clint Eastwood's X-rated spaghetti trilogy, *A Fistful of Dollars, For a Few Dollars More,* and *The Good, the Bad and the Ugly*. It was topped off with *Hang 'Em High,* but, again, this had been an afternoon show when one was reasonably alert and not verging on tiredness. (In 1989, *Star Wars, The Empire Strikes Back,* and *Return of the Jedi* went the rounds as a triple bill in England, but a triple bill that I avoided—one *Star Wars* film per showing was enough for this particular viewer.)

In September, something which I had never encountered before in all my years as a cinema-goer (in the United Kingdom that is) came to pass at Reigate's Majestic cinema—a Saturday all-night "X" certificate horror show comprising five movies: *Tales from the Crypt, The Crucible of Terror, Asylum, The House that Dripped Blood,* and *Vault of Horror*. Starting time was 11:00 p.m. and it finished at around seven-thirty on Sunday morning. Now I *had* come across these kind of multi-movie performances many years before, in 1965 and 1966, when as a ship's steward in the merchant navy I had visited San Francisco and noticed that several films in a single sitting was nothing unusual in the city. In Britain, though, it was extremely unusual and I made arrangements with Neil to get down there on the Saturday night, after a good afternoon's rest and a meal, to experience this rather unique happening. Although an old hand at this game, having countless late-night outings in the 1960s under my belt, this latest showcase, a much-missed part of my cinema life, represented a real challenge.

The old late-nighters comprised two features, which finished around two in the morning. Five films all through the night was a bit of a stamina-tester, even for me. And then there were the flicks themselves. Not any of Universal's golden greats, which would have held my attention without any trouble at all, but a rag-bag of sorts and two of them (*Tales from the Crypt* and *Asylum*) I had seen before. Not to worry. It was too good an opportunity to pass on and might never be repeated (it wasn't, at least not in my neighborhood). So accordingly, after unsuccessfully attempting to get at least one hour's sleep beforehand, the pair of us met outside the cinema at 10:45 p.m. with a fair-sized crowd, strolled into the foyer, purchased our tickets, and chose two seats in the rear stalls.

The Majestic was a very roomy but rather outmoded theater built in the 1930s, the red décor was marked and faded, it had an intangible aroma of mildew and stale tobacco in the air, the seating was hard and uncomfortable, and the floor was stained and sticky. It had most certainly seen better days, but, in its own antiquated way, was quite cozy and at least possessed a degree of atmosphere. At 11:00 p.m. on the dot, the auditorium was plunged into darkness, the heavy green curtains trundled back on squeaky rollers, and *Tales from the Crypt* got underway. Being one of Amicus' more entertaining horror-compilations from the 1970s, it was swiftly followed by *The Crucible of Terror*, a duff mad-sculptor low-budget effort modeled, without doubt, on Warner's *House of Wax*. Though the action took place on Cornwall's north coast, I knew the area like the back of my hand. Therefore, it amused me to mentally jot down the amount of continuity errors in the production, as one location was substituted for another, in the space of a few minutes (even though the action was supposedly taking place in one spot). This was a trait I had inherited from my mother and one that was not appreciated by those who knew me!

After *Crucible* had ended, a much-needed 10-minute coffee break was next on the agenda. The customers filed out, converged in the foyer, and grabbed a polystyrene cup full of the scalding beverage, free of charge, as if the management were saying "Thanks for turning up at this ungodly hour. The coffee is on the house." Making our way back to our seats in the gloom, sipping the burning, but welcoming drink, the lights suddenly went out and *Asylum* commenced, which was another Amicus winner (why couldn't Hammer have delivered this kind of fare to the fans when they were so obviously floundering with their '70s vampire and psychodrama thrillers?). It kept us both awake until 3:50 a.m., when a second interval for coffee was urgently required by the 70-strong audience, some of whom had slumped forward, were probably asleep, or as near as damn asleep. Fifteen minutes later, *The House that Dripped Blood* rolled before our bleary eyes, which was Amicus' four-tale horror omnibus. All of the stories (written by Robert Bloch) took place in a supposedly cursed house, where the sterling cast (Cushing, Lee, Ingrid Pitt) added weight to not-very-scary situations. By now, drowsiness was beginning to make itself felt and I had to give my pal a hefty nudge to prevent him from ending up in the land of nod. I felt slightly yucky myself, as one does when the body's natural habitat, at four in the morning, is bed and not in a cinema watching five horror movies! Thank goodness, I murmured to myself, that we didn't have adverts and trailers to contend with. That would have been too much to bear. The third coffee-break of the night supplied us with yet more caffeine to stimulate the senses (heaven knows what all this is doing to my insides, I thought, as I gulped down the scorching liquid). As we settled back into our seats trying our hardest not to let our eyelids droop, it was time for *Vault of Horror*, Amicus' sixth horror compendium concentrating on five stories this time. Each story was recounted by the main cast trapped in a basement, which turns out to be a cemetery, where all five storytellers are dead, an oft-chosen denouement in these types of movies. At around 7:20 a.m., the night's entertainment came to a close—on came the lights and 70 very haggard-looking patrons stumbled out into the street. Neil dragged himself onto his motor bike and I wearily forced my legs to somehow carry me the mile back to my home, where I collapsed in a heap on the bed to the sound of some distinctly uncaring comments from my other half. Never again, I grunted as sleep overwhelmed me, but this exercise was not to be replicated—it was a definite one-off, put on, perhaps, by the whim of the manager, for whatever reason. In all probability, he was a horror buff, who himself had once sat through dozens of late-night shows and thought he would present one in

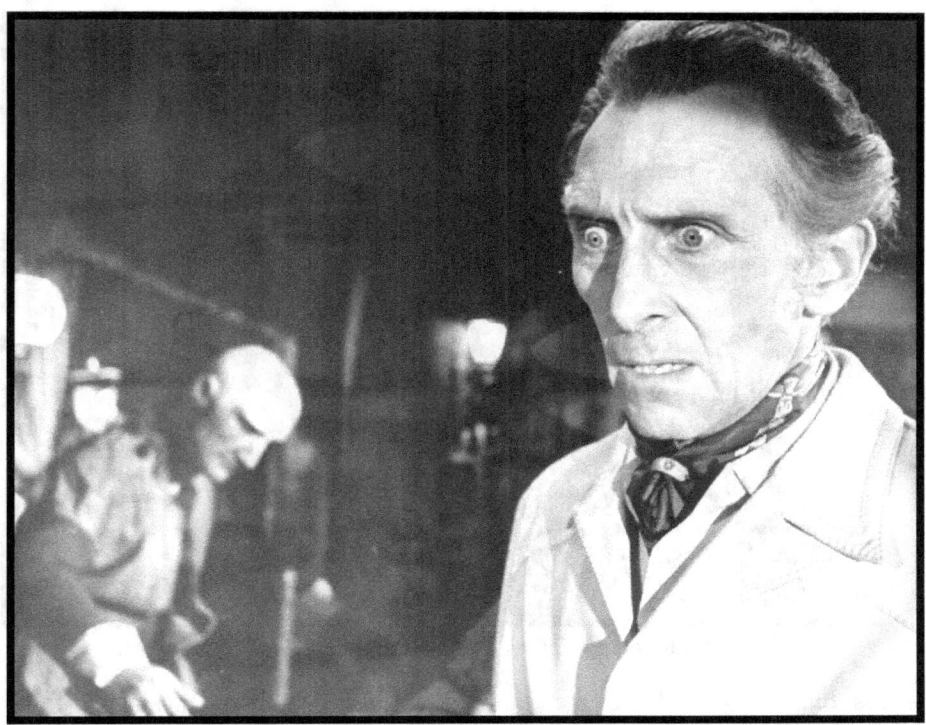
Peter Cushing in the "Waxworks" segment of *The House That Dripped Blood.*

a rather elongated form, whereby to please himself as well as the punters. If so, hats off to him for bucking the system and providing, just for a few brief hours, a taste of what things *used* to be like. (Following this all-nighter, the same cinema screened, commencing at midnight on the coming Saturday, another couple of "X" movies: *Apocalypse Now* and *The Deer Hunter*, a combined running time of 335 minutes together with four intervals guaranteed to test the endurance of even the most seasoned film-goer. I attended the presentation with three friends and this session, together with the previous week's all-nighter, proved to be too much—the outcome being four days off work with a migraine that knocked me flat and a warning from my partner to steer clear of any more midnight trips to the pictures for the sake of my health, as well as hers!)

On a down note, John Carpenter's *Escape from New York* was one of those ugly sci-fi crash-bang-wallop action flicks that proliferated during this period. The director's favorite actor, Kurt Russell, played a one-eyed crook in a futuristic New York and was given the task of rescuing President Donald Pleasance from maximum security prison Manhattan Island. The whole debacle developed into a series of chases as Russell and Pleasance try to escape from the city's crazier elements. There was nothing refined about this picture. Noisy and intolerable, it was a side of the science fiction genre that was in vogue with the latest audi-

Margot Kidder and James Brolin face *The Amityville Horror*.

ences, but was treated with a certain amount of contempt by old lags such as myself, who sat through the whole 99-minute running time and dissected its shortcomings piece by piece, which was much more diverting than the film itself.

On the box, BBC2 was the one station still coming up with the goodies—their "Horror Double Bill" ran a series of '40s gems including most of Val Lewton's output, a second rare showing of *Mystery of the Wax Museum,* and a couple of Hammer horrors thrown in for good measure, which was all captured for posterity on my overused video recorder. As if that wasn't enough, the same channel put on a second mouth-watering package under the heading of "Monster Movie," which was broadcast over a period of five weeks. It included 1933's *King Kong, The Beast from 20,000 Fathoms, Gorgo,* and *Mighty Joe Young*, among others—my collection of video tapes was expanding at an alarming rate!

1982 kept the impetus going in the cinema by commencing with *An American Werewolf in London*, an X-rated horror movie made with wit and intelligence (and a certain amount of dark humor), featuring, as *The Howling* had done, superb transformation scenes and a tragic climax skillfully staged in London's West End. Up in the Capital, Michael Winner's vulgar *The Sentinel* was unaccountably teamed up with *The War of the Worlds,* which still, after 29 years, was burdened with an "X" certificate, despite the fact that it had appeared on television, albeit at a late hour and minus a few scenes that the British Broadcasting Corporation thought might upset some viewers. The double bills continued with *Dressed to Kill* coupled with *The Amityville Horror* and *Star Wars* paired with *The Empire Strikes Back. Creature from the Black Lagoon* (A-rated now) with *It Came from Outer Space,* sole survivors from Universal's golden age of creature-features, had been in circulation, on and off for an incredible 29 years, were allowed one more throw of the dice before they went into well-earned retirement, Admittedly, it wasn't anywhere near as exhilarating as the good old days, but, in this decade, as near to that glorious period as it would ever get, I suppose, and I made the most of what was on offer, even if some of the fare didn't really come up to scratch (or, more specifically, to my own criteria of what constituted as a meaningful motion picture). For instance, *Star Trek 2: The Wrath of Khan* was a noticeable improvement on the elephantine *Star Trek: The Motion Picture,* but it still lacked the drollness and sheer naffness of the television series, and, to be perfectly honest, was a bit of a bind to sit through. Celluloid's ongoing fascination with the Devil, poltergeists, ghosts, restless spirits as portrayed in the humdrum and sub-*Exorcist* histrionics of *The Amityville Horror,* gave birth to Tobe Hooper's *Poltergeist,* an ominous warning of what can happen when developers take short-cuts and build a town over an ancient graveyard. Unfortunately, it forsook old-fashioned chills in preference to a spate of over-the-top special effects courtesy of, no doubt, producer Steven Spielberg. For it pandered to the masses, who clamored for all of the continuous visual battering, and cared not whether the multitude of phantoms, ghouls, evil spirits, and reactivated corpses on display was just, maybe *just,* one grotesque creation too many. Why not stick to one villain of the piece, as producers *used* to. It gave me a headache simply thinking about it and wore me out long before the noisy and predictable climax. *The Entity,* though, was compulsively chilly and more carefully paced about the tale (based on fact) of a woman repeatedly assaulted and raped by an invisible *something*—it ran into censorship problems because of its subject matter and several of England's counties refused to screen it. Once again, I was forced into boarding the train to London to catch the movie at the Odeon in Leicester Square and was suitably impressed by the adult treatment of the material.

I pulled out of seeing Ridley Scott's *Blade Runner* on the advice of a fellow oldies aficionado, who bemoaned the fact that nothing was the same anymore. Unfortunately, this latest science fiction spectacle was just one more nail in the fantasy coffin.

"Why, what's wrong with it?" I enquired over a beer one evening. "The papers are saying that it's not all that bad."

"Yes, well they would, wouldn't they? The whole film looks as though it was shot at night, it's gloomy, almost depressing in a way. Alright, the futuristic vision of Los Angeles is stunning, but it's so bloody downbeat. Don't they make upbeat sci-fi these days?"

"Apparently not."

"And Harrison Ford looks so flaming miserable all the time."

"Bloody hell. Has it got any saving graces?"

"As I said, the movie is OK in parts, in fact the hardware is pretty flawless, but really, Baz, overall it's one long yawn. I'd give it a miss if I was you."

So, as I said, *Blade Runner* was put to one side and forgotten. I eventually caught it on television in 1996 and must admit to agreeing with my friend's scathing comments. In some quarters, this very darkly lit science fiction-cum-detective thriller was hailed as a masterpiece, but not in my quarter. I prefer something that raises the spirits, not lowers them over a running time of two hours. It paid too much attention to the minutia with thoroughly impressive details of Los Angeles in 2019. Also, the director had left the characters out of the scenario, which was a fatal flaw in many post-1970 fantasy productions. It left knowledgeable cinema-goers, like me, hankering for the days when characters *mattered* in film without being secondary to the effects, which they so patently were in Scott's muddy fantasy and others of its kind.

A reasonably productive year came to a close with the release of two fantasy movies at the extreme opposite ends of the spectrum: John Carpenter's "X" certificate remake of the Howard Hawks' classic *The Thing from Another World* (now simply named *The Thing*) and Spielberg's U-rated *E.T. The Extra Terrestrial*. Special effects in science fiction movies had progressed in leaps and bounds since James Arness, in a tattered spacesuit, first menaced Kenneth Tobey and company in a freezing Quonset hut. Carpenter chose to stick closely to the main plot of the 1951 picture, while incorporating many of the ideas in John W. Campbell's story *Who Goes There?* in which the shape-changing alien is never fully described in detail. What's the verdict? After Carpenter's homage to the RKO–Radio original, inspiration was drawn from the same fiery title lettering and the movie kicked off favorably enough. The first rate opening shot occurred with a gleaming spacecraft hurtling towards Earth in a bygone age and was accompanied by Ennio Morricone's doom-laden music, which perfectly complemented the bleak Antarctic snowscapes. During this, the Norwegian helicopter pursued a husky dog over the frozen wastes, while trying to gun it down before the infected animal reached the American base. Following the grisly scene in the dog-pen, where one of the huskies revealed itself to Kurt Russell and *his* company as the alien in disguise, the action became slightly bogged down in the center. This seemed to occur in many similar movies produced from 1970 onwards (which was a sign of sloppy editing, lengthy filming, and lack of directorial self-discipline). Also, the crew of the station was preoccupied with the question of who had been possessed by the alien and who hadn't been to the point of paranoia, and why oh why, in the climax, did Russell have to shout out "Fuck you too!" as he flung a stick of dynamite at the approaching tentacle monster. Fair enough, swearing in movies was now commonplace, but it seemed to me that the producers just had to chuck it in to keep up with current trends. All in all, though, *The Thing* was a solid piece of adult science fiction and horror, although, it was criminally dismissed by a lot of sniffy critics and never achieved the same heights that Hawks' trail-blazer had done 31 years earlier. (Note: When *The Thing* had its British television debut in 1988, all of the bad language had been edited out of the print, as had several of the more gruesome transformation scenes. This included the whole sequence whereby a possessed victim's detached head sprouts feelers and scuttles across the floor like a grotesque spider. Such was the power of the censor even in the late 1980s, a fixation verging on mania. It was very strange when you consider that the movie was screened after the nine o'clock watershed, during the time, when TV companies naively thought, all persons under the age of 18 were tucked up in bed!)

E.T. The Extra Terrestrial was not my cup of tea at all. Never a fan of "U" certificate fantasy fodder or any other "U" film produced expressly for a younger audience, I was put off with the sugary sweetness of it all, despite E.T coming across as quite an endearing little character. John Williams' omnipresent and over-emotional music (another of my pet hates—scores that burble on for the entire length of a picture. Breaks of silence add wonder and heighten suspense) was an irritant. Also, the director's seemingly endless fascination with back-lighting effects began to get under my skin after an hour and the constant close-ups of wide-eyed children in awe of the alien's other-worldly powers proved too much. So I left the ABC in Crawley vowing never to sit through it again. That's what a diet of non-stop "X" films did to you, I suppose, because the film was a massive hit in the United Kingdom and elsewhere, which led me to think that perhaps it was my judgment that was at fault and not the general publics'. But it was still not my cup of tea!

For the second time since 1976, there was no late-night series of horror movies on BBC2, an ominous sign that the British television companies were now falling back on mainstream fare for their audience and, yet again, were turning their backs on the fantasy sector—out of 126 seen in 1982, only 25 were HSFF and many had been on several times in the past: *Psycho*, *Abbott and Costello Meet Frankenstein*, 1939's *The Hunchback of Notre Dame,* and *The Brides of Dracula*. All highly entertaining fodder, granted, but I had seen each and every one of them a dozen times now, both at the cinema and on television. Something new was urgently needed to maintain the interest. Where were the likes of *The Gargon Terror*, *The Unearthly*, Universal's *Creature* movies, Bert I. Gordon's cheapo productions, *Attack of the Giant Leeches*, the Toho *Godzilla* series, the continental horrors of the 1960s, and the P.R.C. potboilers of the '40s when you needed them? Blimey, even a showing of *The Beast of Yucca Flats* would have been something, a variation from the standard run of fare, however awful that variation was! Had they all disappeared into a black hole, never to reappear? (The truth of the matter is that as I write this in 2006, hundreds of these type of pictures which I saw between 1954 and 1970 have never seen the light of day on British television and probably never will.)

If 1980 to 1982 had been, for me, the fairly prolific years of this decade, then the period between 1983 and 1989 was, with one or two exceptions, the most dismal since I first started going to the pictures in 1951. This was partly due to personal problems outside the scope of this book, which prevented me, in one form or another, from focusing my thoughts on celluloid. For I had far too many other things happening in my life to worry about the cinema and what was or was not was on show to the general public. Consequently, my cinema-going habits altered drastically—one movie in 1983 (*Return of the Jedi*), *Sudden Impact* in 1984, the tenth-rate *Indiana Jones and the Temple of Doom* and *Lifeforce* in 1985, *Journey to the Center of the Earth*, *Star Trek IV: The Voyage Home* and *The Hitcher* in 1986, *Aliens* and *The Fly* in 1987, *The Blob* and *Predator* in 1988, and *Batman* and *Star Trek V: The Final Frontier* in 1989—13 films in seven years. Blimey! Way back in January 1965, I had caught 10 movies in five days at The Regal in Redruth! It was a spectacular downfall, but it wasn't my entire fault. The cinema itself was in a state of inertia, was afflicted with dwindling audiences, and the fare on offer was not really of a high enough caliber to pull in the customers, who, for the most part, sat back and waited for the video release. Also, release dates, between a movie appearing at a theater and then appearing in a plastic box in the shops, were becoming shorter and shorter, as well as the tapes becoming cheaper and cheaper.

Jeff Goldblum morphs into *The Fly* in 1987.

On television, BBC2 revived their "Horror Double Bill" in 1983 and went overboard. They screened all eight of Universal's *Frankenstein* classics, two *Mummy* flicks, and Lugosi's *Dracula* with Chaney's *Son of Dracula*. It was a veritable feast that made amends for the dire situation the cinema was finding itself in at this time. In addition to this, the same channel decided to screen their own "Science Fiction Film Festival," which screened 14 sci-fi movies spread over seven weeks on Saturday nights. It was nothing that had not been on before (*The War of the Worlds*, *The Conquest of Space*, *Invaders from Mars*), but a treat all the same. However, that was it from the British Broadcasting Corporation—it was Channel 4 that took up the HSFF mantle for 1984, 1985, and 1986. Some (but only some) of the golden oldies at last emerged from their hiding places: *It! The Terror from Beyond Space*, *Man Made Monster*, *The Trollenburg Terror*, all three *Creature* movies, *I Married a Monster from Outer Space*, *Mesa of Lost Women*, 1958's *The Fly* and *Tarantula*, to name but a few. The video recorder grew red-hot as I taped one after the other, for years after release, the authorities still classed these films as adult material (many were originally certified "X" for cinema release) and most were put on at midnight to avoid younger eyes from viewing them.

BBC television, in 1984, shocked the public with its 110-minute semi-documentary *Threads*, ramming home the harsh realities of what would befall the inhabitants of Britain following a nuclear attack by Russia. Focusing on a family

Darrin McGavin as Kolchak in *The Night Stalker*

in Sheffield, this harrowing saga didn't pull its punches when it came to the grim after-effects of nuclear fallout. For the climax, which took place in a devastated England, people reverted to savagery 10 years later from when the bomb had fallen. The heroine of the tale gives birth to a stillborn mutated infant, being the result of genetic contamination. Repeated once in 1985, but not shown since, this televised film surely deserved a cinema release (and without doubt would have been given an adult rating). But, like so many other television classics of its kind, it has been shunted away somewhere in preference to the blander delights of Doctor Who and similar films.

In 1975, a single showing of Dan Curtis' *The Night Strangler* had appeared on Channel 4 one night and had left a bit of an impression. It was a curious American television movie featuring a pain-in-the-ass newspaper hack on the trail of a serial killer in a spooky underground city in Seattle. Forgotten over the intervening years, Curtis' 1972 *The Night Stalker* appeared on July 25th 1987 on Channel 4 and was followed, a week later, by 1973's *The Night Strangler*. Straight off, I connected with it and remembered seeing the feature-length TV film 12 years previously. Darren McGavin played the rumpled and irrepressible Carl Kolchak: an eccentric, blustering reporter with a penchant for the supernatural, who was the bane of his boss's life (the much put-upon Simon Oakland) and the local police force. In *Stalker*, Kolchak was up against a vampire in Las Vegas and brazenly ignored the orders of the police, who refused to believe his outlandish theories that the person behind a series of slayings was a member of the undead. The police wanted him off the case and out from under their feet. *Strangler* was even better. The action transferred to Seattle, whereby a number of brutal murders, committed every 21 years, led the obstinate but successful reporter to delve into the history of the killings. Eventually, the reporter discovered a century-old alchemist living in the ruins of Old Seattle underneath the main city, who has to resurface at 21-year intervals to drain his victims of blood, thus enabling him to remain ageless. The combination of McGavin's tenacious newshound, Oakland's hilariously exasperated newspaper boss, quirky storylines, cynical slanging matches, and authentic locations was a winner. Therefore, it goes without saying that both of these television features would have made a superb double bill on the cinema circuits. As a bonus, Channel 4 then screened the complete Kolchak *Night Stalker* series that was made in the 1970s after the two full-length features. All 20 of the 50-minute shows took in a variety of paranormal and other-worldly themes including vampires, werewolves, zombies, living manikins, Jack the Ripper, angry spirits, spontaneous human combustion, aliens, and everything thrown into the pot, the effects ranged from the passable to the laughable. Oakland and McGavin were perhaps the best double act of its kind since Abbott and Costello. Regrettably, the adventures of intrepid reporter Carl Kolchak have never been broadcast again on terrestrial television in England since 1987, which is a shame—this is one series that has a cult following in the States and maybe could have had a following of sorts in the United Kingdom if given half a chance.

Returning to the cinema, here are my thoughts on the few movies I had bothered to attend in a half-hearted fashion. *Return of the Jedi* was fantasy for undemanding children—nice to look at, but all style, no heart, and there was certainly no depth behind the unremitting pyrotechnics on display: an array of gadgetry to appease the most ardent *Star Wars* fanatic, which I could not be counted as one. The Ewoks on Endor were dinky little things if you were 10 and under, which I wasn't. Furry and cuddly aliens didn't belong in serious sci-fi and that just about summed *Jedi* up. *Aliens* was a worthy-enough sequel to *Alien*, I acceded, but unfortunately eschewing the unbearable tension of Ridley Scott's masterwork in favor of gung-ho heroics and suffering because of it—the final set-to between Sigourney Weaver and the mother alien was a humdinger, though. *Star Trek IV: The Voyage Home* was a joy, a satisfactory *Star Trek* flick and about time too. Kirk and company time-traveled back to San Francisco in the 1980s to kidnap two whales, whose haunting cries could prevent a mysterious probe from destroying the Earth in the 23rd century. The sheer novelty aspect of the crew at loose in Frisco gave rise to numerous hilarious situations and amusing lines spoken mainly by a deadpan Spock, the inventive story didn't outstay its welcome, and the whole cast looked as if they were having a ball—this was the nearest the long-running series ever came to capturing the spirit of the television show.

Robert Harmon's *The Hitcher* was watchable mainly for Rutgar Hauer's psychopathic hitchhiker, who doggedly pursued motorist C. Thomas Howell, while committing a string of murders. It was a road movie featuring the eternal theme of good versus evil played out with a fair degree of dash. Cronenberg's remake of *The Fly* was a corker, as was Jeff Goldblum in the title role, and it was mercifully short (96 minutes). So the story didn't drag and the stomach-churning effects, which depicted Goldblum's transmutation from man to fly-monster (and in particular his nauseating eating habits), made me wish that I had gone along to the ABC cinema in Crawley on an empty stomach! Like *The Fly*, *The Blob* was a superior "18" certificate remake, embellishing the same plot as the earlier Steve McQueen picture with updated and extraordinary effects. The titanic protoplasmic monstrosity, brought to Earth on a meteor, consumed everything in its path, sucked its victims down plugholes, and stripped them of flesh in seconds—this is what it should have been like in 1958! Arnold Schwarzenegger has starred in some pretty ropey productions in his time, but I truly rate *Predator* as one of his more meritorious efforts—the invisible (for most of the time) alien head-hunter was an original concept, the jungle setting was at least different, and there were some droll one-liners (Arnold on seeing the alien's face for the first time: "You're one ugly motherfucker!"). And *Batman* came up trumps in the superhero chain of feature films, a cracking comic book adaptation, the first and, many would argue, the leader of the franchise with Jack Nicholson going crazily over-the-top (as usual) as the grinning and maniacal Joker. Michael Keaton restrained by comparison, but oozed authority as the Caped Crusader in a remarkably somber and *nour*ish recreation of Gotham City—only Prince's music spoiled matters slightly.

After the critical and commercial success of *Star Trek IV: The Voyage Home*, it was a case of back to square one for *Star Trek V: The Final Frontier*. Kirk, Spock, and company journeyed to a distant galaxy in search, of all people, God, who naturally turned out to be an aging and fraudulent alien in a beard. Cue for plenty of tedious flashbacks as the angst-ridden cast were forced to remember their past traumas—all well and good, maybe, for a television episode, but not strung out over 106 minutes in the cinema. A very poor outing indeed for the well-respected team, which ranked as one of the drabbest in the series—the critics tore it to shreds and the movie did not perform well at the box office.

Of the 13 movies seen between 1983 and 1989, *Lifeforce* was unquestionably the worst, a farrago of a picture and a strong contender for the most misguided big-budget science fiction/horror picture ever to hit the cinema screens. It started impressively with a joint American-Anglo space crew investigating the tail of Haley's comet and discovering a strange female apparently in deep sleep—great, I thought, while mentally rubbing my hands together. This would be something to get my teeth into and with Tobe Hooper directing, Dan *Alien* O'Bannon scriptwriting, and John *Star Wars* Dykstra behind the effects, how could it fail to succeed? But fail it did—big time! As soon as the mysterious female was brought to Earth and taken to London, she set about draining the life-force from the local population, which turned them into withered zombies who then attacked the living. This was a cue for the whole cast to overact like there was

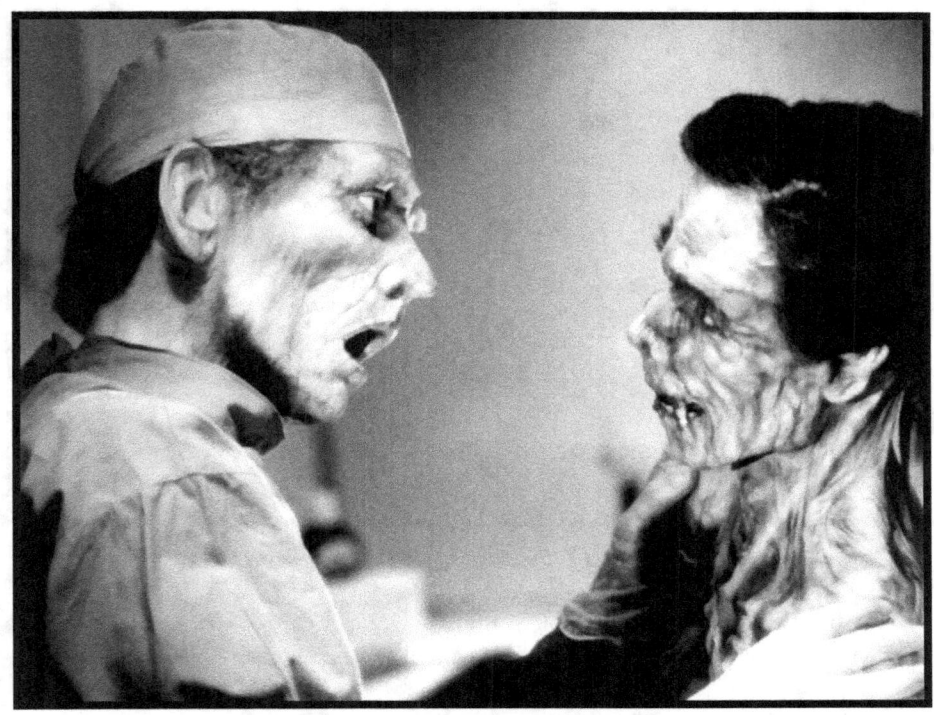
Tobe Hooper's *Lifeforce* left me speechless!

no tomorrow as the police tried to locate the cause of the plague, while doing their utmost to avoid the living dead. This was sci-fi giving way to hysterical camerawork, while the movie seemingly fell apart before the audience's eyes. I left the Odeon in Croydon almost speechless as to how a fantasy feature film could commence so brightly and then deteriorate so alarmingly over the course of 100 minutes, which was something that didn't seem to happen in pre-1970s HSFF. Maybe everyone concerned had been at loggerheads over what kind of a production they were supposed to be creating for the general public. If so, the end result was a bit of a dog's dinner, a severe pasting by the critics and a poor return at the box office were just deserts, some might say.

As usual, it was another delight from the distant past that provided the high spot for me in this relatively barren time in my cinema-going life: A one-off screening of *Journey to the Center of the Earth* at the ABC in Crawley in 1986. On Friday, June 20th, I was scanning the entertainments column in the local paper when the following presentation hit me squarely between the eyes:

Monday 23rd June for 6 days
Tom Berenger in Platoon (18) Doors will open 3:00 p.m.
Saturday 21st June at 10:00 a.m. only
James Mason in Journey to the Center of the Earth (U)

Journey to the Center of the Earth is 132 minutes of enchantment!

"Christ!" I exclaimed. "Look at this."
My partner wandered over and peered at the paper.
"What?"
"Look what's on at the ABC in Crawley tomorrow."
"Yes? So?"
"So I'm off to see it—coming?"
"No I'm not. You and your films. Don't you ever get sick of watching them?"
"No," was the short answer to that question.

Why 20th Century Fox's splendid fantasy was showing in Crawley on a Saturday morning was anybody's guess—quite possibly, the manager could have been a fantasy enthusiast and fancied something worthwhile for a change. Whatever the reason, I rushed over there with Stephen on the Saturday, and, surrounded by a larger than average audience for this time of the day, reveled in every single one of those 132 enchanting minutes. Bernard Herrmann's evocative score not only aroused in me deep-seated emotions for the loss of this type of fare from our screens, but made me realize, not for the first time over the past few years, that composers such as Herrmann had regrettably disappeared from the cinema scene. Music these days lacked the importance it once had and illustrious names such as Hans J. Salter, the pairing of Paul Sawtell and Bert Shefter, Gerald Fried, and James Bernard were a part and parcel of cinema history never to be repeated.

I emerged from the ABC with, I don't mind admitting it, moist eyes and a lump in my throat, perhaps in all likelihood, from an aching for days gone by—it had been 26 long years ago, a lifetime, I ruminated, when me and my mates, still dressed in our school uniforms, had traipsed along one rainy night to Epsom's mammoth Odeon cinema to be thrilled by this picture. So much celluloid had passed under the bridge since then. Unfortunately, the start of the new decade was not going to add to that total, not one iota.

4

1990-1997

For me, 1990 was the rock bottom year and my very own Year Zero. Not one film was seen at the cinema. It was a whole 12 months without a single visit to a picture-house, which for an addict, such as myself, would have been viewed as inconceivable not that far back. I wasn't even aware of what was out there on the circuits, be it science fiction, horror, Westerns, war, or any other format on celluloid. There was nothing much on the box either—34 movies seen and only a handful belonging to my favored genre. Though the one bright spot (some buffs might argue otherwise!) was a first-ever screening of Robert Clarke's infamous B man-into-monster flick of the 1950s, *The Hideous Sun Demon*, screened on Channel 4 at midnight. Well, at least it was a departure from the norm!

The climate in the cinema was undergoing a metamorphosis—it had to if it was to survive in the new and gadget-mad age we were now inhabiting. After my own disastrous 12 months of 1990 and the plummeting attendance figures during the 1980s, when the cinema slid into an artistic decline of sorts (1975 remains the year with the all-time lowest attendance figure in Britain), matters could only, surely, improve in all areas. Small three-in-one theaters, which were once decreed the in thing, were on the decline, as well as the local Odeons and ABCs with their decrepit foyers, uncomfortable seating, below-average sound systems, musty auditoriums, and decades-old interior design. A complete overhaul was urgently needed to restore public faith in the medium of film as a form of entertainment for the masses. It needed to entice and drag back those missing crowds that had deserted in their millions, who were fed-up with anachronistic conditions that may have been acceptable in the 1950s and 1960s, but not in the 1990s. The day of the multiplex had arrived—up to a dozen or more screens housed in a building the size of an office block. It was staggering. There was padded seating with loads of leg-room sloping steeply down to giant screens, surround-sound in Dolby digital, and enough confectionery on offer to feed the proverbial five thousand. Also, inside the multiplex, glossy magazines gave in-depth coverage of new releases, wall-to-wall mini-screens plugged the forthcoming attractions, and film-related merchandising was for sale in kiosks. On hot days, air conditioning was on, as well as central heating when it was cold. The cinema was back with a bang. But none of this would have worked if the product it was supposed to be presenting to the public didn't improve

To me, *Silence of the Lambs* was just regurgitated Hitchcock and Castle!

dramatically as well, and it did, in all areas including HSFF. The 1990s saw a resurgence in cinema audiences on a comprehensive scale as film hauled itself out of the depths of despair and reinvented itself to the benefit of all. Like the new cinemas, the movie was also back with a bang!

I had missed out on an astounding amount of pictures over the past few years for one reason or another, but with a new partner in tow, herself an ardent film fan, I made a determined effort to try to get to grips with whatever was out there, even if it wasn't 40 years old and in monochrome! First off the bat in 1991 was *The Silence of the Lambs*, certified "18" because of its disturbing content (this rating had replaced the "X" in 1984, as the new "15" had done to the "AA"). Was I the only person in the country not to be taken in by this much-lionized serial killer potboiler? I found it to be a regurgitated jumble of everything done before by the likes of William Castle and even Hitchcock himself. Anthony Hopkins was suitably intimidating as Hannibal (the Cannibal) Lecter, but Jodie Foster was too mannered by far in her role as the FBI agent. She was given the task of unraveling his twisted mind in the hope that, on strictly supervised release, he would lead them to Buffalo Bill, a psycho whose specialty was skinning young girls alive. Saddled with a confusing climax in the killer's workshop, the camera wandered all over the place as Foster, seen through the camera's night-vision goggles, tries to escape Buffalo Bill's clutches. This was ultimately a shamelessly contrived and film-it-by-numbers shocker that the continentals used to churn out in the 1960s with far more flair, suspense, and aplomb than was on offer here. Unaccountably, the movie raked in four Oscars, including Best Picture. Without doubt, I was out of synch with the public and *some* of the critics on this one!

Treated with a certain amount of disdain by the U.K. reviewers, who were fast becoming tired of one big dumb movie after another appearing in front of them, Schwarzenegger's adult-rated *Total Recall* appeared. This film was 113 minutes of comic book and machismo brutality. It was a convoluted tale of a secret agent exposing a conspiracy on Mars to depose a dictator, which ended up as an excuse for the one-time Mr. Universe to batter and gun-down hordes of stunt extras against an unrealistic Martian backdrop. Being a coarse and ham-fisted science fiction flick boasting, for its time, a huge budget, the end result was a spiritless and almost unwatchable (and distinctly unlikeable) work of disorganized shambles making full use of the star's limited range of acting.

Misery was a marginally truer adaptation of a Stephen King novel than others before it had been (the finest remains the uncut and 180-minute televised-film of Tobe Hooper's *Salem's Lot* starring David Soul and James Mason, a truly first-class exercise in vampire terror that deserved a cinema release in the United Kingdom), but the picture was too talkative. The interplay between psychotic Kathy Bates and captive James Caan became forced at times, with one piece of harrowing violence that made everyone in the audience, including myself, flinch like mad. (Note: The full-length three-hour version of *Salem's Lot*, an expertly paced shocker that puts a lot of modern-day feature movies in the shade, was televised on ITV in 1987. David Soul played a writer returning to the small town of the title. His visit coincided with the outbreak of a series of mysterious deaths somehow connected to sinister antiques dealer James Mason [marvelous in the role] and his phantom [in more ways than one] partner, a Mr. Barlow. Among a welter of disturbing images, the *Nosferatu*-like vampire was a nightmarish sight to behold, the sequences showing the vampire boy scratching at the window of his friend's bedroom, which really did raise the hackles, and the climax was both grim and fatalistic. This superior chiller was subsequently shorn of one whole hour [the complete end segment had vanished and several of the minor character's scenes had been cut] and was broadcast again in 1996. However, the original edit of *Salem's Lot* was transmitted on Channel 4 [the specialists in showing uncut prints] in 2001, was split into two 90-minute segments, and was shown over successive nights, a reminder to horror addicts of what a masterful piece of work this was, wasted, it has to be said, on the small screen.)

Edward Scissorhands, a charming although very dark fairy tale with a heart-rending ending, featured a cameo by horror stalwart Vincent Price as Johnny Depp's creator, which was his last on film. Depp starred as the pale and wild-haired invention of Price, who sported shears instead of hands, was let loose in small-town suburbia, and was forced to become an outcast by the community, who eventually come to treat him like a leper. Tim Burton's fable borrowed ideas from the old Universal thrillers of the '30s and '40s (the monster as the outcast, persecuted by the villagers), including the original *The Cabinet of Dr. Caligari* and even *Pinocchio* with some success. The public flocked to see it, which proved that the Burton-Depp partnership was a potent draw at the box office.

Terminator 2 rounded off the year, a big and flashy $100 million follow-up to *The Terminator*, whose innovative special effects were much-applauded at the time. Personally, these kinds of movies with their constant stream of explosions, fights, and (apparently) witty asides left me cold. They had a huge fan base, sure, but I wasn't going to be included in their numbers. I fully recognized that this new strain of noisy, multimillion-dollar, and thrill-a-minute picture was the new direction such films took, that a modern audience called for in their product a frenzied slice of action at regular intervals to keep them amused over a running time of two hours plus, but where were the plot intricacies, the subtleties, the different shades, all of which constitute a fulfilling piece of film? Much of *Terminator 2* consisted of a relentless series of set-pieces, expertly manipulated by James Cameron with his foot set firmly on the accelerator, but each trying to outdo the previous one to the point of repetition. Not for the first time could I ever imagine an audience in 1991 sitting through some of the presentations I had endured years ago, which included stuff like *The Incredible Petrified World*, *Curse of the Faceless Man*, *War of the Colossal Beast,* and *Flight of the Lost Balloon.* They had lulls between the action, shoddy effects, rudimentary direction, and wooden acting, but were entertaining all the same in their own archaic way. Today's lot would have walked out in droves. But at least those old pictures had staying power—most of this modern fare was forgotten the instant you left the cinema, being the celluloid equivalent of fast-food. I just couldn't get to grips with this mindless sci-fi fodder. For it didn't float my boat. In all honesty, I probably subconsciously resisted its questionable charms—perhaps, I shrugged, I was simply too old and set in my ways to appreciate the newer variety of HSFF.

At least I now had the opportunity of wallowing in nostalgia by catching up on some of my favorites on Channel 4, who screened another season of late-night goodies in the middle of the year, including *House of Wax*, *The Tingler*, *Circus of Horrors*, *The Return of the Vampire*, *20 Million Miles to Earth*, *Fiend Without A Face,* and 1956's *Invasion of the Body Snatchers.* Consequently, the tape collection mushroomed to a point where it was getting completely out of hand. It took up too much space amid the family photographs and ornaments, so I was asked, politely, to be a little more selective and considerate. "Only record on tape those films you really want to watch more than once," said Jan, trying to be helpful. I appreciated what she was saying, but the trouble was that I wanted them *all* on video, even those I had seen a dozen times or more. But I took heed, swallowed hard, and attempted to limit what delights I decided to transfer to videotape in the future, however painful that might be.

Unfortunately, 1992 was another dip. Only four fantasy movies were seen at the cinema and all four were at small theaters featuring scaled-down screens. These 1970-designed picture-houses were slowly being eased out by the giant 12-screen complexes, but still existed here and there. They were not much different, really, from a home cinema experience in one's living room in 2005! *Star Trek VI: The Undiscovered Country* was a livelier entry in the ongoing *Star Trek* franchise (*Star Trek IV: The Voyage Home* still remains the most enjoyable of the Trekker movies), even receiving tolerable and rather grudging reviews from the nation's critics, who were growing jaded by the capers of a visibly aging starship crew, however distinguished they appeared on the big screen. At least this particular *Star Trek* cut down on the philosophy and leapt straight in with the action, a bonus for the legion of admirers who continued, in the United Kingdom anyway, to make scathing comparisons between the cinema versions and the much-revered television series.

Batman Returns had bucket-loads of imaginative sequences, but in the long run became a drawn-out affair, descending into farce at times and lacking the brooding edge that distinguished the first Batman flick. Danny de Vito went hilariously over-the-top as the Penguin and Michelle Pfeiffer exuded sexuality as a PVC-clad Cat-woman, but the climax tried to cram too much in and outstayed its welcome. It was an omen that the following episodes in the franchise, minus Michael Keaton, would start a downward slide in quality. As for *Alien 3*, set on a remote planet used for housing convicts, repeated usage of the F word does not make for a pleasant viewing regardless of the fact that it was now established practice in 1990s cinema. Never mind the big budget, this turned out to be the worst of any of the *Alien* flicks. It had an unattractive bunch of swearing characters mouthing idiotic lines. They battled a computerized dog-shaped monster in this case. Only Sigourney Weaver brought any semblance of respect to the whole inept business. To cap it all, the ending was almost a direct copy from *Terminator 2*. Where was Ridley Scott when you needed him? Crude, foul-mouthed, and poorly visualized, it was everything the 1979 forerunner wasn't. Really, the *Alien* series should have ended there and then, but of course it didn't—money speaks louder than cinematic art and

Alien 3 obviously made a fair old return at the tills to warrant the series continuing, even though most fans thought that the picture stank

A reissue of *Q, The Winged Serpent* made up for the sorry *Alien 3*, a bizarre and old-fashioned, but nonetheless compelling monster movie concerning a giant pterodactyl-type creature inhabiting the top of the Chrysler Building in New York. It was one of the last pictures of its kind to incorporate stop-motion animation effects. Extremely gruesome, the confusing storyline (part detective, part horror) didn't detract from the Toho-like suspense and an exciting battle at the end between the army and the monster was eye-popping—it could have been lifted right out of several 1950s Japanese monster flicks, a throwback to another age.

Proving that the older movies still retained the power to captivate and entrance, I was pleasantly taken by surprise one weekend when Jan's daughter and her husband paid us a visit. Carrying two cups of tea into our living room, I caught Graham studying my extensive collection of videos, rubbing his chin in thought.

"You've got quite a collection here, mate," he said.

"Yep, I certainly have. All old stuff, though—I'm not too keen on the newer films."

"Hmmm. I wouldn't mind seeing some of these."

"Well, you know me, Gray. I don't lend tapes out. I've been down that road before and had my fingers burnt."

"What do you mean?"

"I let a so-called friend of mine borrow two videos once and never saw the damn things again. Sorry."

"Oh well, I could always come over here and watch 'em."

"You could do that. Ever seen anything like *Revenge of the Creature* or *Tarantula*?"

"No. I've heard of some of them, but, no, I can't say that I've seen any of these."

"Alright, then, fix it up with Sue and we'll make a day of it. I'll put a show on."

His face lit up. "OK, I'll speak to her in a minute."

In a jiffy, Graham had it all sorted out. The date was penciled in for the following fortnight. Graham was 26 and hadn't been around during the golden years, but he read a lot of fantasy and was fully aware of my fanaticism for the '50s brand of sci-fi/horror. So it was arranged that I, as the man with the knowledge, would choose the movies I perceived he might enjoy the most, a cross-section of classics to be viewed throughout the day. In the meantime, the girls would do their own thing, depending, of course, on the state of the weather, which in England you could *never* rely on.

Two weeks later, Sue and Graham turned up at 10:00 a.m. on the dot. I grabbed the beers from the fridge, Graham settled down on the sofa, and I showed him the delights to be put on for his benefit—*Tarantula, Gorgo, The Quatermass Experiment, House of Frankenstein, The Creature Walks Among Us, 20 Million Miles to Earth,* and *House of Wax*. They were diamonds, each and every one of them. Throughout the day, several cans of beer were downed, snacks were provided, the video player grew hotter and hotter, the two women would poke their heads round the door to enquire as to our well-being (they didn't go out—it was raining as usual, so most of *their* day was spent indoors playing Scrabble), and a good time was had by all. Graham was enthralled with the fare on offer. As the pair got up to go later in the evening, he told Sue that the oldies were "really good and no, I wasn't bored." As they drove off, I turned to Jan.

"There goes another convert."

"Lovely." She rolled her eyes. "But no more of *those* films for at least another month. Seven in one sitting is more than enough."

"Yeah, OK," I acquiesced and indeed kept to this promise. An all-day show was stretching it a bit and even I needed a break from fantasy movies from time to time. Besides, one had to be careful not to overdo things. Jan tolerated my interests more than others had done, for which I was eternally grateful. So I went a whole month without watching a single HSFF film. At the end, I was suffering from acute withdrawal symptoms, needing a double dose of *The Curse of Frankenstein* and Terence Fisher's *Dracula* to restore me to my senses!

The fantasy scene on television showed worrying signs of a drop in both output and excellence. 92 movies were watched, a trifling 15 of which were HSFF, including '60s dross such as *Battle Beneath the Earth* and *They Came from Beyond Space*. They lowered the spirits and the only two from the fabulous '50s were *House on Haunted Hill* and *The Monster that Challenged the World*. It was quite clear that British audiences on the whole did not appear to hold the classic oldies in the same esteem that I and others of my bent did. For a fresh generation of cinema-goers was now dictating to the television channels that anything prior to 1970 was considered old-hat and not worth pursuing. Whether this older product was, in terms of cinema history, relevant or not didn't matter. It wasn't up-to-date product, plain and simple. New is what a '90s TV audience demanded—nothing less would do. Video was also making inroads into people's viewing habits so that seeing a film on television was no longer the major event that it once was. Horror, science fiction, and fantasy movies may have formed a major part of America's cultural heritage, where of course the bulk of them were made, but they apparently did not form part of the United Kingdom's. It's no wonder they were pushed to one side and blatantly given the cold shoulder. Hell, not a *single* Hammer film was shown on television in 1992, an almighty rebuff to the one company in the land that had produced a string of classics between 1955 and 1963 and some pretty worthwhile efforts after that. I sighed—there was no accounting for public taste even though, as I was often reminded by my partner, my tastes did not necessarily reflect those of a mass audience. They were too damn peculiar!

On the subject of Hammer, it was reported in the newspapers around this time that a syndicate of business partners from within the film industry was willing to pump a great deal of money into the ailing Hammer company and would breathe new life into what had once been England's prime exponents of top-grade horror melodrama. For starters and to honor the company's first critical and commercial success in 1955, a multimillion-pound remake in color of *The Quatermass Experiment* would be unleashed on the audience of the day, complete with state-of-the-art sci-fi/monster special effects, a mouth-watering prospect if ever there was one. But sadly, like most ambitious ideas of this type, it came to naught. The syndicate pulled out of the project for their reasons and nothing further was heard on the matter. A great pity, this was, because if ever a film company deserved to be resurrected from the ashes, it was Hammer.

Of the 86 movies viewed on the box in 1993, the number of HSFF was unmistakably on the wane—18, with only three representing the 1950s: *From Hell It Came*, *I Was A Teenage Werewolf,* and *The Beast from 20,000 Fathoms*. The remainder was '60s and '70s fodder with nothing whatsoever from the '40s. At the cinema, *Bram Stoker's Dracula* started off the year, a visually commanding retelling of the famous novel that contained some spine-tingling sequences in the first half in Dracula's castle (purloined mainly from the 1922 *Nosferatu*). Then it lost direction after moving the action to London, where Keanu Reeves' dodgy English accent and limp-wristed portrayal of Jonathan Harker did not help matters and Anthony Hopkins was a bombastic Van Helsing. He was nowhere near in the same class as Peter Cushing in the role. Gary Oldman was moderately convincing as the Count, but the unnecessary transformation scenes (which just *had* to be included to cater to a 1990s audience, as they were not featured in the book) detracted rather than added to the tale and the blood-drenched climax left one feeling deflated as well. A brave attempt, I summarized, at doing something out of the ordinary with the old story, but one day somebody would grab the bull by the horns and come up with a Dracula worthy of Stoker's classic tale of the undead, it being a tale that still possessed the potency to chill the marrow, even after repeated readings—a cross between Lugosi's *Dracula* and Hammer's fine 1958 rendition, maybe. It's a pity that it will probably never be made.

It was good to have gotten the turgid *Demolition Man* out of the way, a bone-headed unsubtle sci-fi program about a super cop brought out of cryo-hibernation in the future, who then has to battle to save Los Angeles from corruption and terrorism. Not only does it reinforce the theory that Sylvester Stallone has never made a constructive feature film, but it was typical no-brainer

fodder for the 1990s breed of fantasy buff—loud, clichéd, and wearisome, a parade of explosions and destruction, dulling the senses instead of stimulating them. I made the necessary booking arrangements at the Virgin mega-complex in Brighton in October so that we could take in the latest nationwide smash, Spielberg's *Jurassic Park*. The distributors crowed from the rooftops that the dinosaurs featured in this movie were so true to life that audiences would think they were the real thing—CGI effects had arrived and stop-motion animation was now consigned to cinema's special effects waste bin.

The Virgin was definitely the place to see it—a 10-in-one theater with comfortable auditoriums, giant screens, and ear-splitting sound. It was the latest in cinema viewing, similar to the short-lived Cinerama process in which the screens were so vast that they took up one's complete field of vision to the extent that you could see nothing else *but* the screen. And Spielberg's much-trumpeted monster flick? Well, it's a pity the actors weren't as lifelike as the dinosaurs. The initial entrance of the Tyrannosaurus through the compound's crash barrier was mighty impressive, prompting me and quite a few others to say, almost out loud, "How the hell did they achieve that?", not having a clue as to how computerized animation worked. Men in dinosaur suits, back-projected lizards, and puppets of the *Reptilicus* variety were now banished forever to the scrapheap, but what about that dependable old stand-by, the animated model? Less realistic

they may have been, but even so, the CGI dinosaurs appeared slightly bland by comparison and seemed to lack both the depth and the fantasy element essential to this type of picture. *Jurassic Park* was without doubt cleverly pieced together, but it didn't contain the same evocative quality of, say, Karel Zeman's *Cesta Do Praveku* (stop-motion was actually considered before the experimental footage of a galloping CGI Tyrannosaurus Rex caught the director's eye). And whereas animation maestros Willis O'Brien and Ray Harryhausen were alone in supervising their creations, investing their models with character and emotion, an army of technicians was now needed to bring this super-wizardry to life on the silver screen. It lent a certain coldness to the final product. The dinosaurs apart, the remainder of *Jurassic Park* just didn't measure up to the action. Encumbered as it was, the film contained two ghastly children, inaudible dialogue, a proverbial overweight computer geek, and some incredible banalities in the script that had one squirming in embarrassment ("T-T-Rex? You said we've got a T-Rex?" "Aha." "Say it again." "We have a T-Rex."). Sam Neill added some much-needed gravitas to the proceedings as the paleontologist. Jeff Goldblum shone as a kooky scientist, spouting his chaos theories as all hell broke loose around him. Richard Attenborough's erratic Scottish brogue detracted from the fact that he was the man behind the genetically engineered monsters, and Laura Dern was annoyingly awestruck for most of the time as Neill's companion. What's more, the chase sequences at the end between the raptors and the humans were played out to interminable lengths, which lead to spells of clock-watching instead of screen-watching. Heaven knows what Ray Harryhausen thought about it all. Fair enough, it was a blockbuster that raked in the pounds and the dollars, but that didn't make it any better than *The Valley* of *Gwangi* or *One Million Years B.C.* and it hasn't aged well over the intervening years. However, the days of one or two people laboring for months in the studio moving articulated models inch by inch, filming them one frame at a time, were dead and gone—CGI reigned supreme, whether one liked it or not.

After the brash event that was *Jurassic Park*, I was crying out for a portion of good old horror to bring me back to basics. I found it in *Candyman* coupled with *Cronos*, an unusual double bill going the rounds on the outskirts of London for a limited period. *Candyman* was a superior "look out, he's behind you" shocker concerning a black and hook-handed murderer, a legend in the run-down ghetto in which the bloody events take place. He was brought back from whatever hell he inhabits by victims repeating his name a set number of times. On with it was the Mexican produced *Cronos*, an offbeat vampire-cum-living dead tale regarding an intricate 16th-century clockwork mechanism that enables the creator to live eternally, but at a price, giving him a taste for blood—a dying millionaire finds out details of the device and sets about trying to track it down to prolong his life. His enemies were rival bloodsuckers, who also strove for immortality. Only 23 customers were in the auditorium when I attended the afternoon performance in Tooting Bec, a sorry situation all round, but proof, if proof were needed, that the great horror double bill had had its day. This particular program never made it onto the nationwide circuits. The big chains turned a blind eye to fodder that, in their view, didn't appeal to a widespread audience.

My cinema-going habits for the remainder of the decade centered, with one or two diversions, around the Virgin multiplex in Brighton and then, from 1999 onwards, the UGC complex (now Cineworld) in Crawley. They had plush seating, unobstructed views, mammoth screens, and sound that echoed around the entire auditorium—what more could a cinema-goer want? Well, how about some fun for a start. Fantasy wasn't as important as it used to be and mirroring both the music business and the entertainment industry as a whole, the film industry had cottoned on to the fact that a humongous and untapped market lay out there all ready to part with their earnings and pocket money: The 12-year-olds and under. In the 1950s and 1960s, the "X" and "A" film dominated the circuits to the extent that "U" pictures were hardly ever

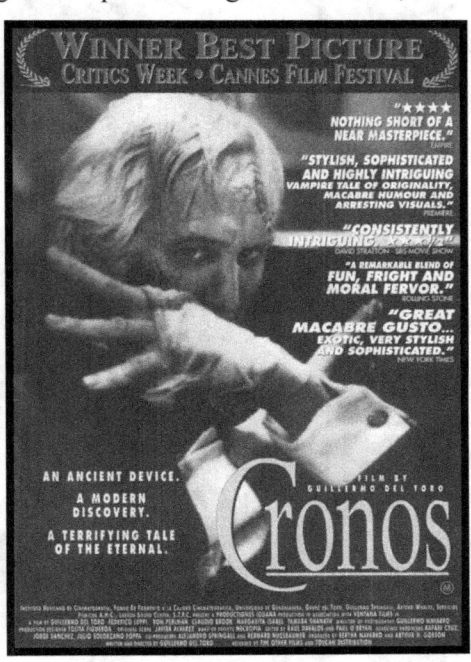

given a look-in—it was the adults who were catered for. The "X" certificate movie triumphed over all others. Now it was the reverse. The PG and "12" certificates proliferated, which were two new classifications in addition to the "U," "15," and "18." In days gone by, innocuous efforts such as *Bride of the Monster*, *The Gargon Terror,* and *Invasion of the Hell Creatures* were handed "X" certificates by the unrelenting British film censor, being judged unsuitable for children, however slapdash their content may have been (and in many cases it was undeniably third-rate!). But times had moved on. Films began to be targeted at the emerging younger audience and, in my view, suffered because of it. To illustrate this change of tack, place Toho's X-rated *Rodan* next to the same company's A-rated *Son of Godzilla*—adult-orientated fare reinventing itself into child-orientated fare. Even the old "U" movies, suitable for a general audience, were somehow produced in a more adult fashion than the new "U" pictures. Take *The Day the Earth Stood Still* (1951) and *This Island Earth* (1954). These were deemed appropriate for everybody by the censor, but they could never in a month of Sundays be classed as juvenile or childish. *E.T. The Extra Terrestrial* and *Star Wars*, both U-rated, *were*, a yawning gulf in audience attitudes spanning 30 to 40 years. Never a great devotee of kiddies' fodder, I found all this extremely depressing. So 1994 was a bit of mishmash with Jack Nicholson starring in unlikely werewolf mode in *Wolf*, which was only partly successful once one had got used to the fact that one of Hollywood's leading actors was actually featuring in a semi-spoof horror movie. Kenneth Branagh's *Mary Shelley's Frankenstein* took its lead from Coppola's *Bram Stoker's Dracula* in attempting to stamp a fresh approach on the Frankenstein tale, but his constantly whirling camera technique, always on the move, destroyed the Gothic aura such a legendary story deserves. Robert DeNiro's monster was faithful to the original

story, but lacked fright appeal. One was left longing for the days of *The Curse of Frankenstein,* which, okay, was Hammer's alternative (and gruesomely stylish) version of the book, but at least packed a punch. Branagh's picture was too worthy and deficient both in the thrills and suspense department. It was lukewarm horror for the 15-year-olds. And to cap it all, Jim Carrey, mugging furiously as *The Mask,* was so far removed from what I classed as entertainment that if I hadn't shelled out £14.00 for the two of us to watch it, I would have walked out of the cinema long before it had finished.

I had high hopes for the remake of *Attack of the 50 Ft. Woman,* but those hopes were dashed on seeing it. The original, of course, epitomized the science fiction output of the 1950s—abysmal effects, risible dialogue, mundane direction, and the proverbial wacky (but typically '50s) poster showing a scantily dressed Allison Hayes bestriding a freeway with an automobile clutched in one hand. It was also classified "X" for adults. You could get away with this kind of product 36 years

ago when huge audiences paid hard-earned money to be entertained by trashy fare such as Nathan Juran's infamous B feature (*Attack of the 50 Foot Woman* was a firm favorite on the Sunday one-day circuit in England during the early 1960s, making it another one of the many "it's so awful it's watchable" movies from that period). But in 1994, patrons expected something a little more sophisticated for their cash so, I wondered, why come up with a '90s version of a '50s sci-fi flick if nobody knew about the 1958 picture anyway and no-one would turn up to watch it. Daryl Hannah took on the Hayes role and was suitably leggy and attractive, but whereas Allied Artists' quintessential slab of old baloney was a classic for all the wrong reasons and was only 66 minutes long to boot, the new film was stretched to 89 minutes. Rated for the kids, it had effects not too far removed from the original, compromising with a happy ending instead of finishing Hannah off. The '50s simply could not be bettered when it came to corny old programs to please the punters. As forecast by the critics, the picture flopped at the box office.

Back on television, only a scattered number of fantasy movies were broadcast (*The Andromeda Strain*, *Capricorn One*, *Planet of the Apes*, *Jack the Giant Killer*) with *Quatermass 2* and *20,000 Leagues Under the Sea,* which were the sole products from the 1950s, making it a wretched year all round on the big screen, as well as the small.

1995 was hardly any better. Only *The Incredible Shrinking Man*, *It Conquered the World,* and *Blood is My Heritage* flew the '50s flag on the box and

there was absolutely zilch from the 1940s, which was fast becoming the forgotten decade, as far as fantasy fare went. At the cinema, *Interview with the Vampire*, an 18-rated opulent and big-budget tale of the undead, was a highly decorous effort with a glamorous cast of bloodsuckers (Tom Cruise and Brad Pitt) and some genuinely shocking moments in between the bouts of *longueur*. *Species* continued the '90s trend of muddled sci-fi, beginning with real promise and then going off on a tangent: H.R. Giger's female alien was the victim of clumsy editing and the stop-motion sequence at the end featured some woeful animation sequences, which was a crime in itself. Giger's Medusa-type she-creature, subsequently shown in an uncut video print, was an eye-opener like *Alien* before it, an original design stuck in a rather messy and, in the end, unsatisfactory picture.

But the undoubted ace in the pack for us die-hard '50s fanatics, in fact one of the *real* highlights of this decade, was Tim Burton's homage to the King of the Awful, *Ed Wood*. Bravely photographed in stark monochrome (it wouldn't have worked in color), this was an affectionate, well-crafted recreation of a period in American cinema. It was a time when umpteen small-time producers/directors churned out films conveyor-belt style—cheapo after cheapo, and countless program fillers, many made in the course of a week and costing peanuts. These movies often featured a once-famous Hollywood star to boost the product—in Wood's case, washed-up and morphine-addicted horror actor Bela Lugosi, who was brilliantly played in *Ed Wood* by Martin Landau, who deservedly won an Oscar for his portrayal. Johnny Depp, as expected, was also in top-notch form as the cross-dressing and angora-loving Wood, carting his band of eccentrics around from one dilapidated set to the next, his hopes, aims, and dreams overriding the sheer shoddiness of his work. The second part of the picture concentrated on the making of the director's most infamous 79 minutes of celluloid, *Plan 9 from Outer Space*, and the movie ended in disillusionment, where Wood never achieved the success he mistakenly believed he deserved. Settling ourselves down in a half-empty auditorium in Brighton's Virgin cinema, I wondered if any of the people sitting around me knew who the hell Ed Wood was, let alone his movies, and whether or not a mid-'90s collection of cinemagoers had any kind of an empathy for this sort of material. Jan admitted to me, before she saw the

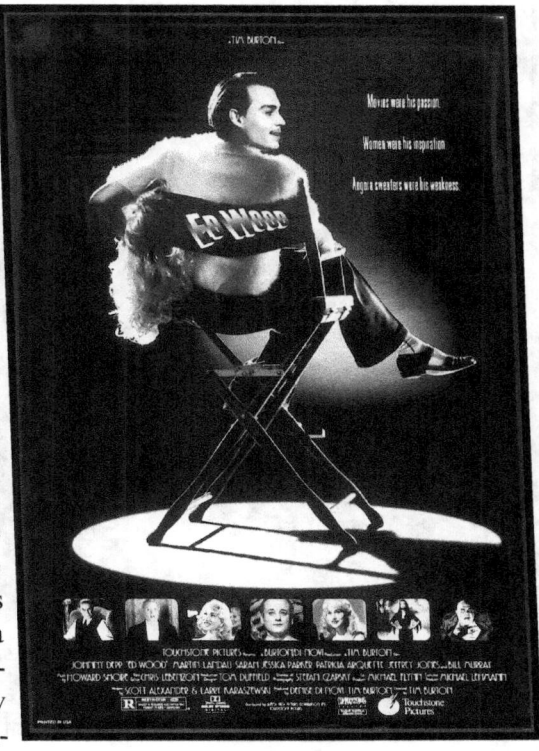

film, that if she hadn't teamed up with me, the name Edward Wood Junior would have meant precisely nothing to her either (David, her son, came with us and emerged a few hours later totally bewildered by what he had just sat through), and this was probably the reason why *Ed Wood* performed so badly at the British box office, despite Burton and Depp being behind it—the film went down a bomb with me, though, and I caught if for a second time three weeks later.

1996 continued the steady and inexorable reduction in fantasy fodder on television, a solitary Hammer production, *The Revenge of Frankenstein, Day the World Ended,* and, again, *House of Wax* sandwiched between the Westerns, the comedies, the musicals, and the war movies. The scene had ground to a halt in the cinema as well—*Independence Day* was the only major fantasy attraction of the year and its "12" rating filled me with a sense of foreboding as we filed into Crawley's UGC to watch it. If Paramount's *The War of the Worlds* had been given an "X" rating, why had this movie, produced on similar lines, been granted a lowly "12" certificate? The answer, of course, was simple—juvenile product for juveniles was the new market force in the cinema. Admittedly the special effects were phenomenal to begin with, but as soon as Will Smith appeared, spouting lines like "We're gonna whop E.T.'s ass," all credibility as a thoughtful alien-invasion spectacle went right out of the window. It became

***Alien Resurrection** **was superior to *Alien 3* but still had little in the way of thrills.**

jokey and flippant, one wisecrack following another and, yet again, the aliens had been blatantly designed using the blueprint from H.R. Giger's original 1979 creation. Completely unmoved by this so-called space blockbuster, a send-up in many ways of the genre it was aping, I yearned for a return of a tasty and old-fashioned "18" certificate sci-fi/horror flick for a change instead of everything appealing to adolescents. It wasn't too much to ask, was it?

In answer to my prayers, a couple of 18-rated movies did turn up in 1997: *Event Horizon* and *Alien Resurrection*, which both, unhappily, were below-par fare. *Event Horizon*, concerning a derelict spacecraft located after many years and the inexplicable force that wiped out the original crew re-exerting its power, which decimated the ship's company who boarded it, boasted, as did most sci-fi flicks of this period, stunning visuals and another strong performance by Sam Neill, but the fatal flaw was the lack of a monster, which left one feeling rather flat after the picture had ended. The fourth *Alien* picture, *Alien Resurrection*, was infinitely superior to *Alien 3* (how could it not be), but by now the original concept behind Ridley Scott's 1979 thriller had been left far behind in another galaxy. The colorful space hardware looked super-duper and Sigourney Weaver was left to carry the day as a DNA-created Ripley, but the movie came across as yet another rehash of dozens of other science fiction films with grisly effects and little in the way of thrills and edge-of-the-seat anticipation of what was going to happen next—the skull-like alien infant was a monstrous creation, though.

Fantasy-wise, 1997 was an odd assortment of fare, ranging from the downright peculiar (*Mars Attacks!*) to the cerebral (*Contact*). Tim Burton's pastiche of the 1950s brand of B movies was highly amusing if, like me, you were lucky enough to have experienced 1950s B movies at the time or shortly thereafter in the 1960s. Perhaps the younger members of the audience (the picture was rated "12") had little idea of what the director was trying, rather successfully, to lampoon, the invading Martians coming across like a bunch of cartoon characters instead of the hostile invaders they were meant to be. *Contact*, however, was a rarity in the effects-driven ethos of the 1990s. It was a slow-moving and intelligent story of an extraterrestrial code picked up by astronomer Jodie Foster and the puzzling journey she undertakes to locate the source of the signal, leading to an ambiguous climax that was similar in vein to the ending of *2001: A Space Odyssey*, an enriching sci-fi excursion that, like a breath of fresh air, tested the mind for once.

Squeezed between these were two absolute clunkers, Luc Besson's *The Fifth Element* and *The Lost World: Jurassic Park*. *The Fifth Element*, like so many films I had seen over the past few years, followed the same old trail, beginning brightly, developing into an overactive farce, and fizzling out like a damp squib. It happened to be the in-flight movie on our return home from the Greek island of Kefalonia in June, but as I didn't use headphones, the story made absolutely no sense as a silent. We therefore went down to the Virgin in Brighton a week later to figure out what it was all about. Unfortunately, 127 minutes later, the story still didn't make a lot of sense, even with sound. Four stone tablets representing the elements are collected by friendly aliens in early 20th-century Egypt, a splendid, imaginative opener which grabbed the attention. Three hundred years in the future, Earth is under threat from an evil ball of fire and it falls on Bruce Willis (in his trademark vest) and the lithesome orange-haired Milla Jovovich (as the fifth element) to retrieve the tablets from marauding lizard-faced aliens in order to destroy the threat. Gary Oldman went completely haywire as the main baddie, but worst of all was Chris Tucker's shrieking and bisexual media star, appearing midway into the picture and completely ruining the general mood. Besson's spectacular-looking fantasy was a very topsy-turvy brew indeed with a garbled script full of mumbo-jumbo, startling effects, a charismatic Bruce Willis (who looked as puzzled as the audience), and an all-over orange sheen of the photography saving the picture from being a complete and extremely expensive dud, but it didn't stop me saying to myself—"What on earth was *that* all about?" Again, I found myself thinking—flashy computer images and one-dimensional characters do not make a good movie.

The second of the *Jurassic Park* movies was a fatuous no-brainer, which, one suspected, director Steven Spielberg had rattled off to fulfill the producers' wishes, having little or no concern with the finished material. Jeff Goldblum was the only survivor from the first picture, dressed in black and looking appropriately glum throughout the entire hackneyed goings-on as he headed back to the Caribbean island. There, it was rumored, the genetically produced

Jurassic Park 2 couldn't stand up to ***Gorgo***.

dinosaurs were alive, well, and procreating like mad—this gave rise to a series of unbroken cliffhangers that irked after the first hour (a case of too many climaxes spoiling what little plot there was). And, I almost said out loud, if one more cast member says "Wow!" after spotting another dinosaur wandering into view, I will personally blast a hole through the screen. The final 25 minutes, with the baby Tyrannosaurus stalking the streets (the director's salute to the monster flicks of the '50s and '60s?) didn't stand up to the likes of *The Beast from 20,000 Fathoms* or *Gorgo*, demonstrating, without probably realizing it, that you couldn't emulate what had been done before. And I for one was glad to leave the cinema before the list of end credits rolled on and on and on—one of the most overblown, inflated, and tedious monster movies I had ever clapped eyes on. At least the oldies were short and sweet and got on with it.

Last up for the year was the new and digitally enhanced version of *The Empire Strikes Back*, with added sequences omitted from the original. All three *Star Wars* films had been given a similar treatment, but I skipped the vacuous first outing and caught the second. Never a lover of *Star Wars* and its incessant merchandising, *Empire*, 17 years on, looked terrific, was still the best of the trio, in my opinion, and profited from the added footage and tighter editing.

On television, the only two sci-fi features from the 1950s shown that year were *Voodoo Woman* and *Return of the Fly*. The river had run dry. Audience research carried out by the main TV companies around this time suggested that the average person or family now required, as an essential part of their viewing schedule, up-to-date movies and not ancient black-and-white artifacts from another era. Echoing the passing of the classic period of horror, science fiction, and fantasy in British cinemas by the close of 1970, 1997 marked the virtual demise of the genre on the box. Apparently, the golden oldies held no appeal or attraction to the vast majority of the television audience anymore unless, of course, you were aged 50 and over. In this case, the *occasional* monochrome tidbit was put on to keep the more senior viewers satisfied and was usually tucked away at two in the afternoon before the kids returned home from school. In regards to HSFF, if one was really lucky, the odd morsel was shoved on at around 10 o'clock in the evening to keep us buffs happy, but more often than not it was something which had been on so many times before that I gave up on it and retired to bed. I had quite enough of sitting up at all hours to watch fantasy fodder in the past, which gave a migraine the next day nearly always as a reaction to these late nights. I was more than willing to sacrifice my health and well-being if, say, *Indestructible Man, Rodan, Monster on the Campus,* or *The Vampire* was to appear instead of repeated screenings of *Forbidden Planet, The Lost World* (1960), and *Dr. Jekyll and Sister Hyde*, but they didn't appear so I stopped watching. (Note: *Indestructible Man, Rodan, Monster on the Campus,* and *The Vampire* have *never* been screened on BBC1, BBC2, ITV1, or Channel 4.)

But now I arrive at a point in this book where a certain amount of repetition begins to creep in because my cine-going routine from 1998 to the present day (2005) remains virtually unchanged. 99% of what I viewed was at the UGC, renamed Cineworld, in Crawley. It consisted of a massive 14-screen complex offering the latest in entertainment luxury, but lacking, as I have mentioned before, the merriment to be had in the old days. The days when a wide and incredibly varied range of theaters presented cinema-goers with visual stimulation on an unparalleled magnitude, when cinemas *resembled* cinemas, not out-of-town hypermarkets all seemingly built to identical specifications. HSFF was, and still is, out on the circuits, but there is a prodigious number that I haven't been bothered with: the horror/slasher teen market (*A Nightmare on Elm Street*, the *Friday the 13th* series, *Scream,* and the rest), the continuation of the *Star Trek* series (come back Kirk, Spock, Scotty and Bones—all is forgiven!), the further adventures of *Batman*, the *RoboCop* movies, the three new *Star Wars* epics, the spin-offs from computer games (*Tomb Raider, Resident Evil*), the *Harry Potter* pictures (avoided on purpose!), the *Matrix* trilogy—the list is endless. Long gone are the days where I felt that I had to see everything on offer, even if it meant attending several different picture-houses in a fortnight. Now, films are on sale in the stores as little as 10 weeks after being screened at the cinema, and in the new format as well, DVD. At last, those clumsy boxes of tapes, tapes that had a nasty habit of snapping or snagging up, could be dispatched to the rubbish bin after they had been transferred to disc. A disc that didn't deteriorate after repeated use and even resembled a miniature can of celluloid because movies are now readily available in digital form after a short shelf-life in the cinema. Television, by and large, has given up broadcasting fantasy fare and very few have an airing nowadays. It's been years, for example, since Universal's *Frankenstein* has been screened on any of British television's four major channels and as for the extensive back catalogue of Allied Artists, Universal International, Warner Brothers, MGM, the small British independents, the continental films studios, American International, Columbia, RKO-Radio, United Artists, Paramount, 20th Century Fox, PRC, good old Hammer, and even Monogram—well, they are never shown. The great British public is not the slightest bit interested in them and they remain oblivious to their existence, for contemporary product is what they desire. Dusty old black-and-white pictures from a far-off age can remain in their cans for all they care.

To illustrate this dearth of classic fantasy fodder on the box in the United Kingdom, let us examine the fate of Universal's own Top 10 on the small screen. 10 top-flight movies that went the rounds in English cinemas for over a decade in the '50s and '60s with great success from both a financial and entertaining the crowds point of view. I put in brackets the number of times these have appeared on the terrestrial networks since television began broadcasting HSFF fare in 1968:

Creature from the Black Lagoon (3)
Revenge of the Creature (1)
The Creature Walks Among Us (1)
Tarantula (1)
Monster on the Campus (zero)
The Mole People (zero)
The Monolith Monsters (zero)
The Incredible Shrinking Man (3)
The Deadly Mantis (zero)
The Land Unknown (zero)

Universal's other favorites: *Cult of the Cobra, The Thing that Couldn't Die, Curse of the Undead,* and *The Leech Woman* have similarly never graced television with their presence. It goes without saying that the British fantasy fan is treated like a second-class citizen as far as the TV companies are concerned.

It is also worth adding that most British film reviewers hold the oldies in low regard. Using four much-loved examples, open any U.K. movie compendium and check out titles such as *The Monster that Challenged the World, It! The Terror from Beyond Space, The Werewolf,* or *20 Million Miles to Earth.* Not even a single one-star rating each, out of a possible four or five, among them and every one slugged off to boot. In fact, some of the critics' comments of these films are so inaccurate that it makes one wonder whether or not the writers concerned actually saw the movies before they were reviewed.

So the pattern remained the same from 1998 onwards, where 12 to 14 trips were made to the pictures over a 12-month period, with only a few HSFF delights included in that year. Any film that I missed, but adjudged important enough for a look, was purchased on DVD and shown on a 28-inch flat-screen television featuring surround-sound.

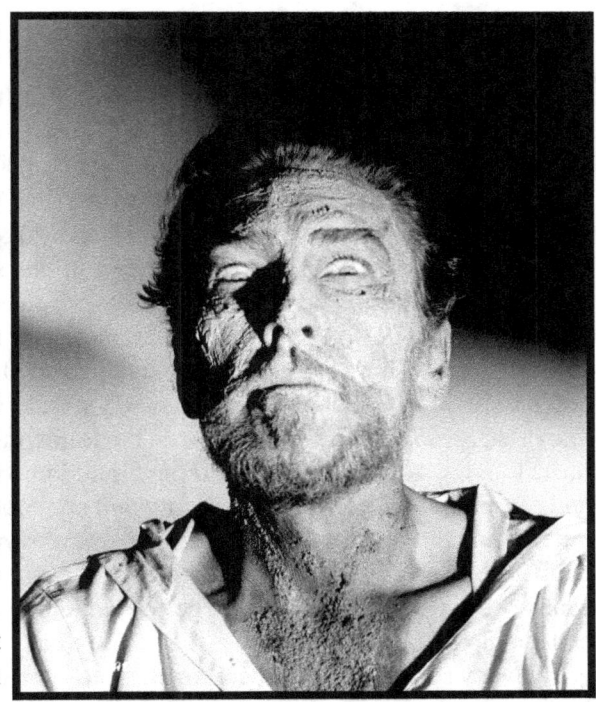

The Thing That Couldn't Die **never showed up on British TV.**

What a stark contrast to the halcyon days of the 1960s when clocking up over 100 movies a year up wasn't anything unusual. It was, after all, the only way of watching films as they were meant to be seen, in their natural environment, as it were. Nothing untoward was allowed to be transmitted on British television (accordingly, in the censor's eyes, little in the way of fantasy unless it was inoffensive fodder along the lines of *The Man Who Could Work Miracles*, no science fiction, and definitely *no* horror) until late-1968 and no device (apart from 8mm film strips and my battered projector) to see them on, but rather, requiring a trip to the Odeon or an ABC.

So let me touch upon the highs and lows of the eight years up to and including 2005 as I cast a somewhat jaded eye at the 20th century's latter-day features and the new century's up-to-date product, some of which was surprisingly rather good, but others unfortunately not so good.

5

AN EVENING OUT—GREEK STYLE (1998)

On our first morning, we are on holiday in Batsi, which is the main resort on Andros in the Greek chain of islands known as the Cyclades. I've already scoped out that not only is our apartment (the Barbara) situated three minutes' walk from the wide sweep of Batsi Bay, but two minutes' walk away from an open-air cinema. A line of posters in glass cases spread out along a white adobe wall announce the forthcoming attractions for the next two weeks. Much to my delight, on Thursday night commencing at 8:00 p.m. is a sci-fi double bill comprising *Men in Black* (which I haven't seen) and *Starship Troopers* (which I have). *Godzilla* is the presentation on the following Monday evening. None of these movies carry any kind of a rating, but I know for a fact that *Men in Black* and *Godzilla* were certified PG in England and *Starship Troopers* a "15." This latter rating has always puzzled me, Paul Verhoeven's retread of countless '50s giant insect movies a catalogue of amputated limbs and decapitations, which is an absolute blast, but a "15"? The United Kingdom's normally strict code of censorship has slipped up here—that picture had "18" written all over it.

"Fancy seeing these?" I ask Jan cautiously on our way to the beach in sky-high temperatures, passing the wall with its array of billboards and waving an arm towards the goodies in question.

"Listen. I came here to relax in the sun, not to sit in a blinking cinema. Can't you just for once forget about horror films? We're in Greece, for heaven's sake."

"Fair enough. I'll make a deal. We'll see these two on Thursday and maybe *Godzilla* on Monday, and we'll catch Nicholson in *As Good As It Gets* on the Saturday. What do you reckon?"

A deep sigh, then "OK, deal. Now come on, the water's waiting."

Over the next few days, we have quickly ascertained that our apartment more or less overlooks this little cinema, where a third of the screen is visible above a few rooftops. Here, there are walls and a rather ornate fountain, the sound (unfortunately for those wishing for a good night's sleep) is clearly audible in English above the racket created by the cicadas, and Greek subtitles are the order of the day. This has enabled us to sit up for four long hours (Greeks, for reasons best known to themselves, love God-knows how many short intervals as part of their viewing habits) on Wednesday watching, or nearly watching, James Cameron's drawn-out, but entertaining *Titanic* through our binoculars. A novel experience if nothing else, but I'm all for seeing any film in odd circumstances or situations and they certainly don't come any odder than this.

Thursday night—on fire from an almost all-over tan, we queue with around 60 locals, by which we are the only foreigners present. As we wait for the blue metal door (secured by a heavy padlock) to slide back on its rollers, my mind

Open air cinemas a very popular in Greece.

drifted back to October 1965 when me and my shipmates queued in similar fashion outside an almost identical theater on the Greek island of Kos to take in Hammer's *The Brides of Dracula* (*You're Not Old Enough Son*: Chapter 12), I smile. Greek cinemas of the open-air variety haven't progressed very much, if at all, over the intervening 33 years if this one is anything to go by. The hatch behind a ragged hole bashed unevenly into the wall opens with a creaking sound, revealing a bearded and swarthy face—this, we assume, is the proprietor in his ticket office. The admission price is handed over: 3,200 drachmas (£5.50 sterling) in exchange for two small pink tickets and the door or more precisely a large metal panel is unlocked, sliding noisily back to reveal the auditorium (if you can call it that) which we wander into. The seating is made up of row upon row of white plastic garden chairs, where all are facing the wall of an apartment block that has a large white square on it—the screen in all its glory. Kids and adults are milling about, chairs are scraped on the compacted dirt floor, and the whole scene, which resembles something out of a vintage British Ealing comedy, is lit by about 40 naked light bulbs strung up along the tops of the walls on cables. As for the sound system, two bulky speakers at the front of the auditorium constitute what passes for stereo or loud, but low-fi.

We choose two chairs near the rear of the cinema as the lights go out (although everything is still visible due to the outside lighting from the numerous apartments and, of course, the vast canopy of the starry night sky). *Men in Black*

appears on the wall in English with Greek subtitles, the stone screen draining the print of color and depth. Fifteen minutes into the action, the movie flickers to a halt. Right in the middle of a line of dialogue, the locals rise as one from their seats and purchase ice-creams, returning to different chairs to those that they left. A blue miasma hangs in the air as some of the older patrons smoke one cigarette after the other. This interval lasts for five minutes. Fifteen minutes later, the same thing happens—the film stops, even though the scene is still playing, most of the audience gets up. More sweets are bought and then the film rolls on. Twenty minutes go by before a third break occurs of five-minute duration, with more chair-swapping, more mobile phones ringing and calling, and more confectionery consumed. Crikey, I muse. It's understandable having *one* short break in four-hour epics such as *The Ten Commandments* and *Lawrence of Arabia,* but *three* in a picture lasting 98 minutes? It is hardly justifiable in my opinion. And the breaks themselves appear any old where—who or what determines them? Finally, the utterly charmless *Men in Black* finishes and I mentally give it the thumbs down. Personally, I detest half-comical rib-takes on *any* genre movie, be it Western, war, or detective thriller, but especially in fantasy. So despite all of its CGI wizardry and freakish alien effects as wise-cracking agents Will Smith and Tommy Lee Jones combat an assortment of mutated horrors causing mischief among Earth's populace, it doesn't cut the mustard with me, for it's a kind of sci-fi *Blues Brothers* that lacks wit and imagination. The type of modern-day blockbuster that earns a fortune in merchandising spin-offs from its gadgetry and stars, but remains an empty vessel as far as any latent artistic merit is concerned.

There are mercifully no adverts or trailers, just another interval before *Starship Troopers* unfolds. As previously stated, this received a "15" rating in the United Kingdom (upgraded to an "18" on subsequent DVD release). Why is it, then, that children I estimate to be as young as seven or eight (there are even a few babies on their mother's laps!) are watching it with their guardians and what's more not batting an eyelid as the giant bugs on the planet Klendathu hack off the limbs of the troopers, drill into brains, and are blown to blood-spattered bits? Perhaps the country where I come from is, and always has been, over-zealous to the point of obsession during its long association with the movie industry and censorship. Who, in the eyes of the State, should see what, and at what age? The Greek youngsters seem to enjoy it, anyway, and notwithstanding the three more mini-breaks, I revel in the picture for a second time. Paul Verhoeven redeems himself after the dreadful *Total Recall* by coming up with an action-packed monster-bug movie that doesn't pull its punches, aimed (refreshingly, for once) at the adults and Greek children!

We leave the cinema at around midnight, the chairs all askew and empty cigarette packets, cartons, and sweet wrappers litter the floor. Climbing the steep steps to our apartment, my mind attempts to formulate a plan to avoid seeing *As Good As It Gets* in those far-from-salubrious surroundings. But my arguments fall on deaf ears. You've had your way, my wife reminds me, and so I'm having mine, meaning that Jack Nicholson is on for Saturday night, but *Godzilla* on Monday night isn't. Two trips to this particular cinema are quite enough, Jan states, and I reluctantly have to agree with her. Therefore, Roland Emmerich's somewhat lumpish monster-on-the-loose flick is viewed from our terrace through a pair of 9x21 binoculars, but only by me—my partner has retired to bed, having been bored silly (her words) by *Godzilla* twice at the cinema, she doesn't share my passion or vigor for a third outing and after fidgeting through all 139 minutes of it, I stagger off to bed at 11:15 p.m. full of one-too-many ouzos. A thumping headache develops and I wonder not for the first time in my 40-year relationship with fantasy cinema—"Is it all worth it?"

6

HIGHS AND LOWS (1998-2005)

1998—The Highs

Very few—Friedkin's *The Exorcist* was given a re-release with an "18" certificate and still proved to be potent viewing after 24-year hibernation from the U.K.'s cinemas. Linda Blair's ravaged demonic features prove to be the equal of any of the current batch of horror movies. Nobody giggled or laughed when I saw it at a packed house in Crawley. And *Godzilla* contained some extremely impressive CGI effects—it's just a pity that the movie was not classed as adult material, rated PG, suffered from murky photography (rain was pouring down in every single scene—why?), had an unmelodic and pointless score (didn't they all these days), and was lumbered with a trite script. But it was still enjoyable enough, although not up to the stature of Toho's more powerful "X" certified 1954 original. *Starship Troopers* I have covered in the previous chapter, an action-packed and incredibly grisly space opera where, for once, the furious pace, especially in the second half as the troopers took on hordes of giant bugs on a nearby planet, made for exciting viewing.

1998—The Lows

Lost in Space—a travesty of the cult '60s television series. The quirky cardboard-ness of the TV program giving way to ear-splitting, flashy video-type histrionics, an unsympathetic Robinson family complete with an unruly and pretty horrible punkish daughter, a lamentable Dr. Zachary Smith (overplayed by Gary Oldman), and a confusing and nonsensical ending. It made for seriously painful viewing. *Deep Impact* had the hoary and well-worn plot of a meteor heading towards Earth and the attempts of a band of mercenaries to stop its progress. Their mission partly fails, leaving a fragment of the meteor to hit the planet. The effects were surprisingly well below the decade's high standards, the righteous script patronizing and sickly sentimental—*When Worlds Collide* did it so much better in 1951!

1999—The Highs

Mighty Joe Young—at last, a respectable remake for a change, featuring some superb CGI effects—a welcome guest appearance by Ray Harryhausen (the man behind the RKO 1949 classic) and a happy ending for the giant ape. Slightly old-hat for 1999, granted, but none the worse for it, and Joe Young himself was an outstanding (for Disney) creation. He was almost Kong-like in his actions, movements, and general demeanor. *The Sixth Sense* may have been deadly slow in some scenes for a ghost thriller, but was meticulously structured. The trick ending caught most people by surprise, and Bruce Willis turned in his usual solid performance as the troubled child psychoanalyst attempting to delve inside the mind of Haley Joel Osment, who insists that he can see ghosts all around him. *Gods and Monsters,* like *Ed Wood* before it, probably only appealed to a minority audience. But this moving tribute to director James Whale's troubled life during the production of *Bride of Frankenstein* was a gratifying experience for all those lovers of the early Universal horror pictures and everything that they entailed. And let's not forget another Saturday morning screening of *Jason and the Argonauts* at Crawley's ABC—a high in anybody's book.

1999—The Lows

Gus Van Sant's rehash of *Psycho* was an unmitigated disaster. Shot scene-for-scene in color (a big mistake here!) from Hitchcock's exalted 1960 classic and utilizing Bernard Herrmann's legendary soundtrack as well, it was a misguided experiment in moviemaking that ultimately failed on all counts. Anyway, who could possibly better Anthony Perkins' Norman Bates? What, I thought, was the director's objective in going to all the time and trouble making it if, as expected, it would be ridiculed by the press—which it was! As for Stephen Sommers' *The Mummy*—the "12" rating said it all. It was a combination of an Indiana Jones action man and a *very* mild horror film (and absolutely nothing to do with either the Karloff 1932 classic or Hammer's colorful remake, whatever some critics inferred). The uncomfortable mix of comedy, wisecracks, and mummy-myths, together with the onslaught of special effects at the film's climax, became inharmonious and tiresome in the extreme. Oh for the days when a menacing Christopher Lee emerged from Hammer's studio swamp in 1959—style and measured pace nowadays in this modernistic fare was nowhere to be seen. Rounding off the year, the much talked-about *The Blair Witch Project* was 75 minutes of handheld amateurish melodramatics. It had a few eerie moments I'll agree, but the countless shots of a leafy woodland ground and a rather confusing and flimsy climax made for unsatisfactory cinema—a clear case of hype over material.

2000—The Highs

After a 28-year period of anonymity in the United Kingdom, *A Clockwork Orange* was let loose on a new audience with an "18" certificate. A few snooty critics gave it a pasting, stating that the intervening years had not been kind to Kubrick's disturbingly brutal vision of the future, but the opening hour still packed one hell of a punch. Malcolm McDowell's cocky and vicious Alex was one of the screen's most distinctive and underrated interpretations of a definitive anti-hero. (It was during a shopping expedition with my daughter, herself a budding film fan, that I was asked, out of the blue, "Dad. Can you get me in to see *A Clockwork Orange?*" I allowed myself a wry smile because, as quick as a flash, I recalled asking my father the same question in May 1960. I pestered him, at the age of 13 years and 4 months, to be allowed to see Hammer's X-rated *The Mummy* when two years and eight months under the legal age in England to enter a cinema and watch it. My father surprisingly agreed to my request and assisted in helping me breach The Crescent's forbidding foyer, enabling me to experience one of Hammer's all-time classic offerings. And now here was Vanessa, 40 years later, after the same favor and, ironically, *her* age was 13 years and 4 months as mine had been, but the difference being that she was four years and eight months under the legal limit, the movie she so desperately wanted to see classified "18." With my past track record of sneaking in to see scores of horror films when years underage, it would have been hypocritical of me to refuse her wishes. So on the following Saturday we entered Crawley's UGC cinema, my daughter, on advice from her unlawful father, made-up heavily. I purchased the tickets and we waltzed through the barrier without any questions being asked. Unfortunately, I had forgotten how explicitly violent and sexually disturbing Kubrick's picture was, so I was a might embarrassed on exiting the UGC, shame-faced at having subjected Vanessa to what one haughty critic stated was a "sci-fi/psychodrama appealing to thugs and delinquents." When it came to light many months later that I had introduced my daughter to the world of the "18" certificate movie without anyone else's prior knowledge and that the "18" in question was *A Clockwork Orange*, I was lambasted about the episode for a very long time afterwards. My father and *The Mummy* had a lot to answer for!

Pitch Black caught both England's film critics and the public totally unawares, sneaking onto the circuits virtually unannounced and trouncing most of the year's other big-budget releases at the cash registers. A cast of unknowns stranded on a remote planet battle flesh-eating nocturnal aliens, who emerge from their underground lairs in their thousands when the planet's two suns go into eclipse simultaneously. It was fast-moving, had nail-biting action, and was a tad '50s in feel. Also, it featured some dazzling color photography in the opening daylight scenes, this was immensely entertaining sci-fi fodder, propelling Vin Diesel as the baddie-cum-goodie into instant stardom. *What Lies Beneath* was a somewhat contrived supernatural-cum-horror chiller with perhaps one climax too many (a trait of modern-day moviemaking), but well-acted by Harrison Ford and Michelle Pfeiffer with some moments of unease worthy of Hitchcock himself. And *2001: A Space Odyssey* was re-released in a spruced-up print for a limited run. It still looked amazing on the giant multiplex screen, shining like a beacon among the welter of new releases, a testimony to the amount of sweat and toil that Stanley Kubrick had put into his landmark science fiction picture.

2000—The Lows

There were several this year, including *Mission to Mars* (a '50s-style effort short on pep and zing. The film was let down by its soppy ending and was another lightweight exercise in how *not* to make a memorable sci-fi blockbuster), *X-Men* (one more in a series of comic book heroes brought to the big screen, which by now were becoming very similar and all directed at computer-mad teenagers), *Hollow Man* (*The Invisible Man* updated—exceptional effects ruined by a frenetic and lousy climax), and *Hannibal* (the continuing adventures of the cannibalistic serial killer in a plodding and dreary follow-on to *The Silence of the Lambs* and a rare misfire for director Ridley Scott).

Two remakes hit the circuits destined to disappoint the well-versed fantasy buff, *House on Haunted Hill* and *The Haunting*. The first was 18-rated, a blood-drenched take on the old 1958 Vincent Price thriller, Price's mansion was now the disused Vannacutt Psychiatric Institute for the Criminally Insane presided over by mad Geoffrey Rush in Vincent Price mode. Five strangers are invited to spend the night there—if they survive, $1 million is theirs for the asking. Unfortunately, Rush was no Price (although bearing a passing resemblance), the gory theatrics were interminable and suspense was lacking. In fact, the picture was screwed-up in every department. Come back William Castle, I mentally yelled at the screen towards the closing minutes, all is forgiven!

I was warned off going to see *The Haunting* by a friend of mine. "Don't go, Baz, you'll hate it," said Trevor one morning at work. "Why?" I enquired, intrigued as to *why* I should hate it. "Take my word for it, you will," he replied. Needless to say, I didn't take his word for it, but I should have done. How could a remake of MGM's incredibly nerve-tingling ghost/horror thriller not warrant a visit? Easy—the "12" rating was the answer. Jan de Bont's retread was for the kids, yet another exercise in Hollywood gadgetry gone berserk as Doctor Liam Neeson invites three insomniacs to a haunted house so that he can carry on with his research into the psychology of fear. Nothing was left to the imagination, so one's imagination ceased to function in a way, unlike the Robert Wise original, which had your creative powers working overtime trying to figure out just *what* was behind those doors and walls causing all those banging noises. I yawned my way through it, exiting the UGC demoralized at what I had just sat through—an atrocious remake in every sense of the word. In fact, it was an insult to all those producers/directors of years ago, who knew perfectly well how to manipulate and scare an audience into submission without millions of dollars spent on fancy and unconvincing special effects.

2001—The Highs

Jurassic Park 3 is, in my view, the best of the series and that was down to the fact that it was shot in a similar style to a 1950s monster movie. Though short (92 minutes), it leapt straight into the action without the need for any boring preambles. None of the chase scenes were spun out to unending lengths as in the previous two outings, the dialogue was snappy and the dinosaurs looked fierce and imposing. Also, the reliable Sam Neill (who only agreed to star in the movie if the finished product improved dramatically on the crummy *The Lost World: Jurassic Park*) turned in a fetching performance as the world-weary paleontologist coerced into returning to the dinosaur-infested island under false pretences to search for a missing boy. The first of the epic *The Lord of the Rings* trilogy appeared at the end of the year, *The Fellowship of the Ring*, while director Peter Jackson had abandoned plans to film a new version of *King Kong* (which would eventually surface in 2005). Never an admirer of this type of mythical fantasy and not having read J.R. Tolkien's mammoth novel, I was nevertheless bowled over by the action, effects, and beauty of the New Zealand scenery. It was enough for me to anticipate the second installment, which was due out at the end of 2002.

Highlight of the year for me was *The Others*, a superbly orchestrated ghost story with minimal effects and a riveting performance by Nicole Kidman, who pulled out all the stops as a disturbed mother attempting to protect her two children from a disquieting presence in her gloomy and fog-shrouded old mansion. The traumatic and unexpected climax delivered a real wallop. I for one was surprised at the leniency of the film censor in this instance, granting *The Oth-*

ers a "12" certificate—this was a "15" movie if ever there was one.

The much-underrated *The Ninth Gate* was another good-un. Ostracized director Roman Polanski returned to the fantasy genre with this carefully paced occult chiller starring the dependable Johnny Depp as a shady book dealer. He is given the job, by a millionaire collector specializing in satanic writings, of locating the two remaining copies of *The Nine Gates of the Kingdom of Shadows*: a manuscript, so legend tells, that was written in league with the Devil. Depp has to compare the two copies, if he can lay his hands on them, with his paymaster's to see which the authentic copy is. The book's nine engravings house a riddle that

can unlock the gates to hell. Over the ensuing 132 minutes, Depp's colleagues and contacts start dying like flies, a mysterious woman teams up with him, who is not all that she appears to be, and the startling climax reveals the true and evil secret of the book. The movie was scoffed at by some critics who claimed that it didn't contain enough fireworks to keep an audience happy. Comments such as these were, sad to say, a lamentable reflection of how film reviewers in a few of the dailies had been brainwashed into the new way of doing things, movies like *The Ninth Gate* pooh-poohed because they were considered old-hat. Subsequently, despite another in a long line of unconventional, but telling performances by Depp, classy direction by Polanski, and a story that gripped from the onset, the picture was not a success in the United Kingdom. There really was no accounting for the public's (and the critics') taste, I thought, as we exited a half-empty auditorium after being enthralled by it—a compelling and quite creepy thriller ignored by the masses.

2001—The Lows

Yes, against my better judgment, I was pressurized by my sister in going along to sit through (or tolerate) *Harry Potter and the Philosopher's Stone*, the subject matter of which interested me not one iota, falling asleep through at least 30 minutes of it and striving to stay awake to the bitter end. Child's fantasy on a feverish and hyped-up scale, which is utterly foreign to my particular tastes, as my sister should have realized! Why I bothered to go and pay good money to see *The Mummy Returns* after the abysmal *The Mummy* I'll never know, but I did. In fact, I found it to be marginally better than the first picture—but only just. Silly, sub-Indiana Jones action flicks do not appeal and the torrent of special effects on display at the expense of characterization and plot numbed both the brain and the senses. Spielberg's overly ambitious *A.I.—Artificial Intelligence* turned out to be the director's first poor effort in years, commencing interestingly enough with an unnerving Haley Joel Osment playing the android child given to a bereaving couple to make up for the loss of their son (short-lived—the other child recovered). Then it plunged into tedium in the garish '70s style middle section (when Osment meets up with Jude Law and a motley collection of androids) before regaining some ground in the final segment, a frozen world in the distant future controlled by aliens, who discover the little boy and grant him one wish for a whole day, *Pinocchio*-style. Cut out the center and you had a reasonable sci-fi outing with a message—as it was, the film rambled on for far too long towards its foregone conclusion.

2002—The Highs

Donnie Darko—the undoubted high of the year was an unexpected hit with the critics to boot. Jake Gyllenhaal shone as the troubled youth, who may or may not have been the victim of a terrible accident. He was given 24 hours to live out his wishes before he vanishes into eternity by a giant ghostly rabbit from another dimension. To some degree it was inscrutable thought-provoking, and with a deeply moving ending, this was the surprise crowd-puller of 2002. The second of *The Lord of the Rings* movies hit the circuits in December, *The Two Towers*, introducing the scheming and schizophrenic Golem and a wealth of new and unusual characters (more ambitious in scale than the first picture, especially the spectacular battle of Helm's Deep. This remains the leader of

the trilogy, where there is not one single redundant moment out of the whole three hours).

From Hell may well have been the umpteenth retelling of the Jack the Ripper legend, but this version had more blood and guts than most. As witnessed by the "18" certificate, the grimmer side of London's East End was graphically depicted and any film starring Johnny Depp has to be worth the price of a ticket. His performance as the opium-smoking detective on the trail of the Ripper is exemplary as always. *Ghost Ship* was a lively haunted ship thriller, commencing in grisly fashion when a ship's passengers are slaughtered wholesale and then continuing splendidly with a gang of salvage operators boarding the derelict liner, who fall prey one by one to ghostly and murderous visitations. And a somewhat unorthodox zombie flick appeared out of the blue, British as well, *28 Days Later*, dealing with a diverse group of citizens on the run from a highly contagious virus transmitted by bodily fluids that decimates England, turning its victims into rabid zombies. Slightly amateurish to look at, with overactive use of the camera, it nevertheless galloped along to its gross-out climax.

2002—The Lows

Signs—the pace was deathly slow and almost grinding to a halt at times in M. Night Shyamalan's "crop circle/the aliens are coming" sci-fi picture containing a lot of hidden messages relating to Mel Gibson's fragile state of mind, although there were admittedly some sinister episodes to unsettle the youngsters as the aliens attacked Gibson and his family in their remote farmhouse. The director's signature sting in the tale climax saved *Signs* from coming across as a lot of pretentious codswallop, but even so it didn't put a stop to the critics' barbed comments, intimating that Shyamalan was useless with the nuts and bolts of film craft. His only concern would be how to end his movies on a revelatory note. The film was also burdened with yet another new British certificate, the "12A," meaning that kids could now get in to see the previous 12-rated pictures with an adult. In other words, there was more wishy-washy fodder for the youths to see at the expense of the poor old persecuted grown-ups. Another remake, the dimly photographed *The Time Machine*, was not too bad compared to others of this decade with an inventive-looking time machine itself. However, MGM's 1960 original remained the superior flick in all departments, particularly the special effects, which were a disappointment in the new film. And a shabby British effort, *The Bunker*, attracted flack from the critics, well-founded for a change. A group of soldiers hiding out in a bunker during the last war are terrorized by the living corpses of men, who have died and been buried in the surrounding woods. The movie degenerates into burlesque as the squad is massacred one man at a time. Hammer in their prime would have produced a classic spine-chiller with this material. As it was, the film fell to pieces long before its 90-odd minutes were up.

2003—The Highs

Ridley Scott released a director's cut of *Alien* containing scenes deleted from the 1979 version, which together with a spot of prudent trimming, meant that the overall running time had become shorter by a couple of minutes. The result was a slightly more superior picture that still held its own 24 years down the line. The teen horror flick *Final Destination 2,* by and large, passed me by, but I trotted along to see this one out of inquisitiveness and was pleasantly caught up in its twists and turns, not to mention the outlandishly blood-and-guts deaths and a genuinely horrific car pile-up sequence that had me driving cautiously home afterwards in third gear! The final *The Lord of the Rings* epic, *The Return of the King*, was the big Christmas movie in the United Kingdom—awe-inspiring to participate in, especially as we were stuck in the front seats during a sell-out performance. It was a let down by its prolonged seven to eight climaxes, as though Peter Jackson had been unsure as to how to bring the whole nine-hour enterprise to a close.

2003—The Lows

Solaris was one more in a continuous flood of remakes, very few of which bettered the originals. This was a pedestrian, although wonderful to look at, version of the 1972 Russian space epic. It was so sluggish in its delivery that several members of the audience decided to take an early bath and leave the auditorium long before the picture had ended—I must admit I was tempted to join them because basically the new *Solaris* ended up by being as dull as ditchwater. And *The Core* was *Unknown World* meets *Journey to the Center of the Earth*, a glossy overblown slab of hokum about a disparate group of scientists sent to the Earth's core to stabilize it before the planet cracks up—mediocre gung-ho heroics with only adequate special effects.

As for the soulless *Van Helsing*, words nearly fail me. Could this honestly have been, as one reviewer had the temerity to suggest, a tribute to Universal's series of classic 1930s horror movies? *Ed Wood* was a tribute—this stinker wasn't. An uninterrupted outbreak of corny-looking CGI effects (flying vampires, the mummy, Frankenstein's monster) to keep the kids amused, hence the "12A" rating. This load of old bunkum, which actually, to me, summed up everything that was wrong with the current-day brand of HSFF fare, must have had Boris Karloff, Bela Lugosi, Lon Chaney, and the long-departed producers and directors of Universal International spinning in their graves. Hugh Jackman, as so many others did at this time, jumped onto the Indiana Jones bandwagon as the vampire killer with an arsenal of fancy weapons at his disposal to combat the monstrosities on display (Peter Cushing—where were you in our hour of need?). There was more wit, imagination, and artistic merit in the opening five minutes of *Bride of Frankenstein* than was on display in the whole of *Van Helsing*. On leaving the cinema after it had mercifully finished, I was saddened by the one thought—has the genre really sunk to this level or is the film I have unfortunately just sat through a one-off disaster? (The jury is still out on that one!)

2004

This was a very lean year indeed for the horror/fantasy connoisseur and I only managed to catch three movies on release. *The Day After Tomorrow*, Roland Emmerich's disaster-laden action flick about the consequences of global warming on the Polar ice-cap and the catastrophic sequence of events. which followed, contained the usual barrage of effects that ranged from the sublime (a tidal wave hitting New York) to the ridiculous (a host of tornadoes decimating a city). All characterization was kept to a minimum (as in Emmerich's other two blockbusters, *Independence Day* and *Godzilla*), meaning that one had little empathy with any of the leading players. After showing promise in *Donnie Darko*, Jake Gyllenhaal came slightly unstuck in this picture as the young man trying to survive in a frozen New York as his father treks through the wastes to locate him. The remake of *The Texas Chain Saw Massacre* was an adequate slasher time-filler, but was nowhere near as gut-wrenching as the 1974 movie. It only really appealed to those gore fanatics, who were not all that bothered with subtleties, just out-and-out confusion and unremitting violence. *Saw*, on the other hand, was much grittier and down to earth and rated "18," a glossy and stomach-churning horror thriller concerning a maniac who devises ingenious ways of dying for his victims. Two men waking up in a washroom chained to the walls realize that they are next on his list if they cannot manage to escape in six hours. Full of nightmarish and macabre slayings, director James Wan really did lay on the gore with a trowel, but with verve and style. The bombshell in the final few minutes took everybody by surprise—this was an accomplished shocker that delivered the goods in spades for a change.

2005—The Highs

Spielberg's *War of the Worlds* was the summer blockbuster in the United Kingdom and a return to form for the director, making it a spectacular reworking of both the H.G. Wells novel and George Pal's 1953 classic. It was coura-

geous of Spielberg to incorporate many of Wells' ideas, however old they were, in the design of the alien war machines, giant tripods blasting the populace with ray guns, using baskets to house the captured humans, and the invasive red weed also put in an appearance. Tom Cruise, one of Spielberg's main choices for a leading man, turned in his usual measured performance. It was a nice touch also for us fans of Pal's action-packed trail-blazer to catch a glimpse of Gene Barry and Ann Robinson, the two leads from the original, at the end, even if it was only for three seconds! *The Descent* was a cracker, bringing forth rave reviews from the critics ("The best British horror movie in years"). Director Neil Marshall piled on the tension with relish as six women go potholing deep down into an uncharted cave system in the Appalachian Mountains, only to discover a colony of blind, leprous, and carnivorous humanoids lurking in caverns hundreds of feet below ground, who proceed to pick them off one by one. Bloody and claustrophobic, hence the "18" rating, and with a savage twist in the tail (not to mention the shock accident at the beginning), this was intelligent, well-written horror fare, matching anything to come out of Britain and America over the past couple of decades.

Finally, after nearly three years in the making, Peter Jackson's 188-minute, $207 million version of *King Kong* hit the screens in December. Give Jackson his due—even to attempt to somehow revamp and recapture the spirit of one of the silver screen's greatest pieces of celluloid, a picture that was part of cinema folklore, so that it would appeal to a modern-day audience would have been an extremely tall order for any director. But the final outcome, after all the publicity and media coverage prior to its release, took the wind out of the sails of the cynical film critics in the United Kingdom. It was a virtual homage to the 1933 classic including in-jokes to the original, scene-by-scene reconstructions (Kong on his mountain ledge with Ann Darrow, outlined against a setting sun, the fight with the Tyrannosaurus), a breathtaking depiction of 1930s New York in the Depression era, pristine photography, winning performances from the leads (though not, I hasten to add, in the same league as the legendary trio of Fay Wray, Robert Armstrong, and Bruce Cabot), and a thoroughly believable Kong himself. Retaining the beauty and the beast motif, the prehistoric backdrops, a totally scary Skull Island complete with hordes of goose-bumpy creepy crawlies, the overgrown jungle from hell, and the immensely moving climax, Jackson's labor of love would never, in a million years, embed itself into the psyche of a mass audience in the 21st century as *Kong* had done in 1933. After all, Cooper and Schoedsack's movie had been knocking around for over 70 years and had been seen by generations of cinema-goers. But at least Jackson avoided all of the pitfalls evident in the woeful 1976 version and came up with probably one of the greatest remakes of all time. It's a real pity the original Max Steiner soundtrack couldn't have been utilized (part of it was given an airing in the theater sequence) and several scenes quite frankly failed to measure up to the sheer visceral power of the 1933 *Kong*. Notably, the giant ape's rather lame first appearance and the prolonged, not all that dramatic, breakout from the theater. The picture also suffered from sheer over-length, one or two characters in the first hour being superfluous to plot requirements, and there were far too many dinosaurs that tended to overload the senses (modern directors take note—less is more!). The Empire State building climax, however, was simply stunning and expertly choreographed. Audiences by 2005 had become blasé over fabulous special effects, expecting the usual thrill-a-minute ride to keep their attention spans going (what is wrong with slowing the pace down now and again?). So one couldn't possibly expect a film like *King Kong* to create the same kind of impact the original did in the 1930s, but regardless of that, Jackson *almost* achieved the downright impossible—equaling (and I know it's sacrilege to say this, but try thinking about the film in its own right and in its own time) one of the genre's most revered and best-loved monster movies.

2005—The Lows

There were only two films, including a teenage rerun of *House of Wax*, an excuse for a bunch of youngsters (including the delectable, but dumb Paris Hilton) to wander into a strange and empty town to become victims of the madman running a local wax museum. As a nod in the direction of the Vincent Price classic, the villain was called Vincent, but when unmasked, his features were nothing like as hideous as Price's had been 52 long years ago. Why oh why couldn't they have tailored the picture to suit, just for once, adults and not teenagers? Banal teenage dialogue, a non-existent soundtrack, and a ridiculous climax in which the whole town goes into meltdown proved for what seemed like, to me, the umpteenth time that modern-day Hollywood was completely unable, or unwilling, to better a golden oldie—Warner Bros.' classic 1953 spine-chiller won this contest hands down.

After years of discussion concerning who should direct and star in the cinema version of Andrew Lloyd Webber's *The Phantom of the Opera*, a certain amount of anticipation was felt when booking to see it, but unhappily, it simply wasn't worth the entire wait. While the songs remained intact and sounded as impressive as ever, Gothic mood and tone was little in evidence—it needed a stronger contrast between the grandiose music and the atmosphere of shadowy terror generated by the Phantom himself. As it was, the masked menace was distinctly not menacing. The relatively unknown leads were okay, but not commanding enough to carry the story and the photography a tad murky, although the set design of the opera house was sumptuous and decorative. It unexpectedly failed to ignite the box office and capture the public's imagination. Perhaps they should have employed John Travolta (as was rumored) in the title role after all!

THAT WAS THEN—THIS IS NOW

Sunday 20 August 1961

    I, Chris, Pete, and John pull up on our bikes outside the lofty and weathered façade of Dorking's Embassy cinema. It's 1:15 p.m. and a sizeable crowd is milling about outside, waiting for the doors to open in about five minutes. We wheel our steeds round to the side of the building, where a length of chain is threaded through the spokes and the ends padlocked together. It ensures that our bikes will hopefully still be there when we leave the cinema, be it early or late. Strolling to the front of The Embassy, we spot the prominent billboard for today's one-day presentation, a real humdinger of a double bill—*The Deadly Mantis* and *Rodan*. Both films were certified "X" Adults Only. Now only five weeks ago, we managed to get in here to see *The Creature Walks Among Us* coupled with *Tarantula*, both rated "X" (as most of these American horror films are) and were followed by two "A" movies: *The Mole People* and *The Monolith Monsters*. So this is our third visit to the place in a very short space of time and why not—The Crescent in Leatherhead still refuses us entry to adult fare. Therefore, we might just as well concentrate our efforts on a cinema that shows, without realizing it, a little benevolence to its underage patrons. All of us are aged 14 and a half, legally not entitled, in the authoritarian climate prevalent in the United Kingdom, to have the privilege of sitting through one of Universal's classic giant insect thrillers and one of Toho's most colorful monster productions. Even though we have been successful twice here before (we are just old enough for the "A" movies, but still receive searching looks), we cannot, and will not, take the place for granted. So we join the queue as it files in through the swing doors and are still apprehensive at the thought of facing that intimidating ticket kiosk. Afraid that we will be found out to be the impostors that we are and expelled into the street, we notice the stills to both movies behind the glass cases, which look very enticing. We also spot a group of kids, who, judging by their appearances, are no more than 12 years old and looking extremely nervous at the daunting task of breaching The Embassy's barriers in order to experience the wonders that will shortly be unfolding inside.

    As the tallest of our little group of horror addicts, the task of obtaining the tickets falls squarely on my shoulders and I therefore approach the glass booth cautiously with my mouth drying up and my body as taut as a bowstring. In a steady voice (this isn't easy, given the circumstances), I ask for four two shilling tickets. The elderly woman in the kiosk stares up at me for several seconds (it seems like several hours), reels off four little mauve tickets, and exchanges them for the money. We are in! Creeping over to the confectionery counter like the four guilty schoolboys that we are we buy, for sixpence each, a little

cardboard-type program listing the presentations for the remainder of August and the first two weeks of September. Declining the cartons of orange, we amble into the enormous auditorium, grabbing four seats in the rear stalls. The place fills up quickly as more and more people enters to take their seats. The stuffy auditorium was badly lit and a musty smell assailed the nostrils, an odor no doubt from the thousands (or even millions) of customers, who have sat here over the decades. The décor is faded red, threadbare in places, many of the seats are scuffed and ragged, and the screen is hidden behind heavy brown curtains. Music from Cliff Richard and The Shadows blares out, while wreaths of blue smoke hang in the air as people begin to light up. Between every second seat, in every aisle, is a small metal ash-tray that digs into your knees if, like me, you are approaching the six-foot marking. Leg-room is at a premium in these cinemas. Packing them in is the name of the game and this particular theater can easily take in several hundred people, perhaps more, I quickly estimate, if you include the balcony or circle, as it is sometimes called. I pray that nobody taller than myself plants themselves in front of me. The auditorium is virtually level and a person of above-average height can obscure part of the screen, thus spoiling your viewing pleasure. Chris fires up an untapped Senior Service, passes it to Pete, and then lights up three more, handing one to me and the other to John. As I drag away, I recall that *Rodan* was paired up with *Tarantula* under the heading Big Monster Double Bill!! over in Fetcham not so long ago, while *The Deadly Mantis* was on with *The Looters* at The Crescent in June—now they are paired up here. I'm slowly beginning to wise up to these programs. The movies in question pop up at one cinema here, another there, all the time exchanging partners to keep the punters on their toes. My reverie is interrupted by the lights going out, plunging the auditorium into an almost impenetrable blackness, where only the faint glow from the exit signs is visible in the dark. The curtains roll back with a rattle and a creak as a shaft of brilliant white light cuts across our heads to the screen, the certification details to *Rodan* coming up, then the big red title lettering accompanied by the giant reptile's thunderous squawk is shown. For the next 79 minutes, we are entertained by our first Japanese horror flick and a thrilling one at that.

The movie ends, the curtains close, and as the dingy lighting comes on, I lean across to the others.

"Bloody good film, that."

"Yeah!" come three replies, in unison.

"We going to watch it again, Baz?" This is from John.

"Yeah, you bet we are."

The lights go out almost immediately, the curtains jangle apart, and three minutes of advertisements are shown, mainly consisting of poorly photographed stills and some scratchy film of local business premises. Then the trailer moves to what's on next week and in this case, *The Guns of Navarone* is revealed, which is proving to be a big hit in England. This is followed by the "A" trailers to two "X" films, *The Black Sleep* and *Four Boys and a Gun*, which is next Sunday's one-day attraction. I whisper to Chris next to me that I'm definitely going to see them and he agrees to join me. The curtains close again for all of 15 seconds, then the clatter opens (who is working the damn things, I wonder) as the certification details flash up to the main feature (This is to certify that the following film has been classified for Adults Only: *The Deadly Mantis*. X). The giant Universal International logo appears, *The Deadly Mantis* gets underway, and the next 79 minutes of pure black-and-white monster heaven has us pinned to our seats in awe.

After the end credits are over, the lights flicker on and Cliff Richard belts out another hit, but we're staying put and going nowhere, and neither is a large part of the audience—these two movies are too good to sit through only once and we have decided to have second helpings. Something we normally do anyway. It doesn't seem to worry the Embassy's management. They never come round, checking on who's here, who isn't, and who shouldn't be. The ice-cream lady walks slowly down the aisle to the front of the screen, a queue immediately forming to purchase a tub of the stuff, but we remain in our seats. Experience has taught us that if you are caught in the queue when the lights go down, it is virtually impossible or at best extremely tricky, to find your way back to the stalls in the dark, leading to much blundering about and trampling over people's feet as you try in vain to locate your proper seating position. Suddenly, the auditorium is thrown into eternal night as *Rodan* commences its second showing of the day. The ice-cream lady, a tiny figure outlined against the lower left-hand corner of the screen, has her face illuminated by the light from her tray. Toho's superior monster picture and Universal's superior giant insect picture are both lapped up for the second sitting and at around 7:35 p.m. we finally exit The Embassy, unlock our bikes, and cycle back along a near-empty

A24 to Leatherhead, where we all promise to meet up next Sunday to catch *The Black Sleep.* The Crescent's presentation on the same Sunday is *The Werewolf* and *The Big Heat,* which we have to ignore. It's pointless even thinking about seeing *that* double bill until such time we somehow work out a way to persuade the cinema's management that we are of an age to see "X" pictures, even when we aren't whenever that might be.

Saturday 9 July 2005

"Fancy seeing *The Descent* on Saturday?"

"Might do. What's it about?"

"Well, apparently the papers are saying that it's the best British horror film in years. Neil Marshall has directed it. He did *Dog Soldiers* a couple of years ago. It's about a group of women who explore some caves and encounter a load of flesh-eating creatures hundreds of feet below the ground."

"Hmmm. Sounds good." (Jan acknowledges the fact that I am the household expert in this field.) Shall we book?"

"Yes, we better had. At least we'll get a decent seat."

During Friday evening, Jan telephones Cineworld's booking line and orders two seats on her credit card for the 11:30 a.m. performance, our preferred time of the day with no kids hanging around, no hassle with parking, and is cheaper, too. After the noon showing the price of a ticket almost doubles from £3.95 each to £6.00 each after 12:00 p.m.

Saturday morning—we drive over to Crawley and park in Cineworld's massive car park, then walk up to the colossal façade of the 14-screen complex, posters advertising the current presentations lined up side-by-side above the automatic doors, not really visible to the punters, but who cares about posters these days? There was a time when they used to be the essential ingredients of a trip to the cinema. Almost works of art in their own right, posters were powerful promotional tools to draw the crowds with unbelievable (and very often misleading) slogans to match—but not anymore. Likewise the stills—there aren't any. The modern-day cinema buff isn't interested or probably not even aware of what they are or used to be. We enter through the automatic doors, obtain our tickets from the card machine, hand our tickets to a youth in front of a roped-off barrier, who doesn't look old enough to shave and who mumbles that it is free seating. We enter the red-carpeted foyer, noticing that our choice of movie is on at screen 5. Heading for the pick and mix, we pass the drinks, the countless bags of sweets, hot-dogs, the crisps, the nachos, and the popcorn. We choose two small bags of assorted confectionery. That will do us fine. A free copy of the glossy in-house magazine is taken from a rack and we make our way over to screen 5, our ears assaulted by a cacophony of noise from about 20 small television-type monitors positioned around the foyer that broadcast non-stop (and ad nauseam) future attractions.

The auditorium for screen 5 is one of the largest of the 14, yet still seats only around 300 people. The seating is arranged on a steep slope and faces a giant screen *not* hidden behind curtains! We grab two seats near the back—comfy with plenty of room to stretch out and no ash-trays. Smoking is banned. The air conditioning is on—a cool breeze is felt fanning our faces as we settle ourselves down. Five minutes later and there are about 23 customers in the brightly lit auditorium, several looking vacantly at mobile phones, or, in some cases, a portable electronic game. The lights gradually fade and the adverts come on, 17 (I time them) very long deafening minutes,

which bore me rigid and most of the punters too judging by the glare and muted, but audible ringtones from their phones—what are they doing with them, I ask myself. Is it really necessary to have the bloody things inside a cinema? The adverts mercifully over and done with, it's time for the trailers to show the forthcoming releases. Trailers last three to five minutes each, which practically give the whole plot away. Why see the film, watch the trailer instead. Another 12 minutes drag by (that's 29 stupefying and eardrum-bursting minutes since the lights went down), the trailers finish, and an FBI notice is flashed up warning of the dire consequences befalling any persons foolish enough to tape the picture while it is playing. Another warning included in the countdown to the start of the feature tells people to switch off those annoying phones and finally the certification details appear ("18" in this case), followed by *The Descent*. Rather irritatingly, a small light is in my left-hand peripheral vision. One of a row of recessed lights is lit and situated down both sides of the auditorium, which are dimmed, but never go out (as stipulated by the law and fire regulations). You can see quite clearly around you and one or two people still (despite that warning) staring at those tiny LCD screens instead of the big screen in front of

109

them. Christ almighty, why do they bother to come, I say to myself. And how on earth can people sit there with those huge tubs of popcorn on their laps? There's enough in one of those containers to feed a family of six and that doesn't include the gallon of soft drink used to wash it all down with. I sigh heavily. It is best not to get too stressed out by it all—that's the way it is these days. Notwithstanding these distractions and the uncomfortable decibel level of the Dolby sound system, I enjoy the film immensely, a superbly directed and gory exercise in clammy terror with a well-rounded set of characters. It has genuinely loathsome monsters, inspirational underground locations, and a surprise shock ending. Yep, the film is definitely four out of five for this one. The movie ends, the lights come on, and everybody leaves the auditorium—no sitting around for second helpings in 2005, unless, of course, one buys another ticket.

Leaving the complex and making our way towards the car, we discuss *The Descent* in detail, as we always do. It must have made an impression on my wife as her fingernails had made an impression on *my* right arm. Neil Marshall's gore-laden horror flick has obviously done its job! But, as I drive out towards home, I reflect on the way the cinema has evolved to this 21st-century level. It's all rather sanitized nowadays, this going to the pictures business. One pays by credit card for one performance only (no co-feature), there are tons of unnecessary merchandise, no stills or billboards, the posters are blithely ignored, people are seemingly disinterested in what they are paying good money to be entertained by, and the movie you have watched is out on DVD in three months' time. Sometimes I wonder if it's worth all the bother, time, and expense of creating a major motion picture in this day and age, but one thing is for certain—I thank my lucky stars that I was around during that period in time when going to the pictures and all that it entailed was an occasion that meant something to the great British public, because it certainly doesn't appear to mean a great deal now.

8

REFLECTIONS (2006)

Fifty-two years ago, I sat sandwiched between my parents on a rock-hard seat in the cavernous, pitch-black, and chilly auditorium of Leatherhead's Crescent cinema, a nervous seven-year-old trembling in fear as *Devil Girl from Mars* unfolded itself in all of its cardboard glory before my startled eyes. Fifty-one years later, I sat next to my wife in armchair-like seats with acres of leg room in a steeply inclined and non-smoking auditorium bathed in the warmth of in-house heating. A line of miniature lights ensured that everybody could see everybody else (health and safety measures even pervade the cinema) and I watched a $200 million digitally enhanced *King Kong* romp across a giant screen in Dolby surround-sound. There was the occasional little square of radiance from a mobile phone being an unwelcome intrusion, which is a sign that today's audiences are not altogether wholly transfixed by what's showing in front of them—21st-century consumerism and a wealth of electronic gadgetry in the home has given people the attention span of a gnat.

The Leatherhead Crescent Cinema in the good old days.

So have things changed for the better over five decades? I personally think not because the days when the cinema was the be-all and end-all of one's leisure activity was a thing of the past. Many moons ago, films ran on the cinema circuits for years and years—now they are on sale in the supermarkets three months after their release dates. There is no need to pay a visit to the local multiplex to see each and every one of the current releases that take your fancy. For you can buy the latest movie on DVD a few months down the line. The 1930s and 1940s were the decades for classic horror, the 1950s the decade for classic science fiction, the 1960s the decade notable for the rot setting in. Horror, science fiction, and fantasy now is a very hit and miss affair. Blockbusters such as *King Kong* vie with American revamps of Japanese and Korean horror (*The Grudge*, *The Ring*), teen-slashing flicks (*Jeepers Creepers*, *Cabin Fever*) and 12-rated watered-down versions of unforgettable originals (*The Haunting*, *Planet of the Apes*). With one or two exceptions, the great days are well and truly over, as is the high-spirited "I'm really looking forward to seeing this" aspect of actually popping along to the pictures. One longs for that period 40 years ago when one was *not* subjected to a deluge of advertising wares on display, whose ears were *not* deafened by 15 minutes of thumping loud and never-ending adverts. When trailers were exactly that—trailers, not potted versions of the complete film, when one was *not* informed that the FBI (yes, even in the United Kingdom) would prosecute anyone found to be unlawfully taping the current presentation as it was playing, and when one could stay in the auditorium all afternoon and evening without being blocked out when the show was over. No, the times when we 14-year-olds stayed seated for hours on end in the stygian surroundings of Dorking's Embassy, glued to three showings in a row of *Teenage Frankenstein* and *Blood is My Heritage*, are consigned to the attic of my memory. How I miss that lengthy and rewarding spell in my cinema-going life, I sometimes think when walking up to the gargantuan glass and concrete edifice that is Crawley's Cineworld. Antiquated in many ways it may have been compared to today, but I gained far more pleasure from outings to the cinema 40 years ago to what I do now. Consider this—100 plus trips a year between 1961 and 1967 wasn't uncommon. Now it's 12 to 14 maximum. If this sounds like a lament for the past, so be it. I unashamedly admit that it is, but count myself extremely blessed to have experienced and to have been involved, as a paying customer, those heady years between 1954 and 1970. The present-day way of doing things cannot hold a candle to it.

Well, it's pretty absurd when you think about it for me to carry on moping about these matters and feeling dissatisfied with the state of the scene as it currently stands and, as my wife often points out, is it *really* all that important? After all, now you *are* old enough son! No, I suppose it isn't in the natural order of things. This is 2006, not 1966. Here's where I take a break—excuse me, I'm just going to slip a DVD of *20 Million Miles to Earth* into our player and indulge myself in 82 minutes of nostalgia for a change.

9

A CONVERSATION—THE OLD VERSUS THE NEW (1)

"Hey, Baz, you seen *Hulk* yet?"

"No."

"Oh, right. I saw it on DVD on Saturday. As a matter of fact, I was a bit disappointed with it; it took bloody ages to get going. Why haven't you seen it, then?"

"Actually, I bought *Hulk* on video for my daughter's son last year and he stuck it on when we were on a family outing round there and *he* wasn't too impressed with it either. Mind you, Luke takes after me—he likes the old horror movies, I'm always doing copies of my tapes for him onto disc. I did three double bills for him last month. Hmmm—oh yeah, he had *Gorgo* and *The Beast from 20,000 Fathoms*, *It! The Terror from Beyond Space* and *First Man into Space* and, er, *The Curse of Frankenstein* and *The Mummy*."

"Christ. How old is he?"

"Eight."

"Doesn't he get nightmares watching all that stuff?"

"No. Tracy says he stays up all night riveted to them. Some of them he's seen over and over again as well. Just like I used to, in fact."

"So you've watched some of *Hulk* then?"

"Well, yeah, bits of it. Why didn't you like it?"

"I told you. The film took ages to get going, it just dragged on and on. That bloke, David Banner wasn't it, well, he should've changed into the monster right at the beginning, you know, turning green and ripping his shirt off, that would have made it better."

"Yes, but what about the build-up?"

"What about it?"

"Well, you've got to have build-up, you just can't jump straight into the action, otherwise you end up with over two hours of action, action, action and nothing else. And television is just as guilty in this respect as the cinema these days as well. Take the new Doctor Who for instance. In the '60s and '70s, each story generally ran over six episodes, 30 minutes each. Now, it's one 45-minute slot per story or maybe two. Everything has to be crammed into those 45 minutes to the extent that storylines don't make that much sense, all you get is one monster after the other, chasing the Doctor about. No build-up, no careful plotting, just one quick scene after another."

"So?"

"I don't know. You lot today, you've got no bloody idea, have you. Why is it you have to have something going on every single minute? Hang on, I'll tell you why—spending hours on computer games and Play-stations has done it. It's addled your brain-boxes. Hell, in the old days, it took *ages* for a monster to appear in a sci-fi film. I'll give you an example" (pause for thought). "Right. *Behemoth the Sea Monster*—that movie is about 80 minutes long and you don't get to see the monster fully until about 50 minutes of plot development has taken place. And when it does appear, you appreciate it more."

"That's boring. How could you sit through something like that?"

"Well, first of all, it's not boring, it's called good cinema. Anyway, they didn't have the budgets in those days to come up with anything better. And if you reckon that was boring, you should see some of the drivel I did sit through on many an occasion. The thing is, these modern films, they're all noisy and flashy, like video games, no pace, no music and, let's face it, who's going to remember any of them in 10 years' time?"

"Who remembers *your* old films?"

"Believe me, mate, a lot of people do—trouble is, they're all Americans. Nobody in this country seems to give a hoot about them. Have *you* ever seen any old black-and-white American horror films, by the way?"

"Actually, a mate of mine has got one on video, about a giant spider on the loose in the desert. Gets bombed at the end. "

"Ah. Sounds to me like Jack Arnold's *Tarantula*. One of my all-time favorites. What did you think of it, then?"

"Mmmm. Magnified spider, wasn't it. Quite good, I suppose."

"Quite good? It's a classic!"

"OK, then, what did *you* think of the new *War of the Worlds*?"

"It was alright, but have you seen the original?"

"Yep. Got it out on DVD the other week."

"And?"

"The new one was better."

"Why?"

"It didn't hang around, did it, like the old one did. The tripods were fantastic, in the old film they just hovered on beams. And all they did was to come to Earth in cylinders, not on bolts of lightning. Tom Cruise was good in it as well, so were the aliens."

"Yeah, Cruise was OK. I'll pass on the aliens, though. What about the music?"

"What music?"

"Exactly! You never, ever get a proper soundtrack these days. Years ago, you had tremendous music in films. Now you would have difficulty in remembering a single bloody note. And I'll tell you another thing—Spielberg's *War of the Worlds*, like most of these new remakes, just hasn't got any lasting power. Yeah, I'll concede it's better than most of today's other releases, but, I don't know, it's difficult to put a finger on it, it's almost as if they've all been churned out on a massive conveyor belt, as if someone is saying, right, here's *War of the Worlds*, knocked out in a year, now let's move on to the next one. They're all a bit bland and lackluster, aren't they? It's different now—I don't think that all that much love, care, and attention goes into these pictures, I really don't. Blimey, the original *The War of the Worlds* was shoved out on general release 14 years after it was made, and people *still* queued up to watch it. Plus of course it was an "X." Kids under 16 weren't allowed to see it. That's the trouble now, of course. Every flaming science fiction film ends up with a "12A" or PG rating, it *all* has to be for the kids."

"What made the old movie an 'X' then?"

"Well, those scenes where the soldiers are running around on fire for a start. Any person on fire in a film—that was it. 'X!' Distress on someone's face—'X!' A bloody injury to the body—'X!' They were produced for adults only, that's why in the 1950s and 1960s, most films were X-rated."

"Huh! Well, I admit the old version was pretty good, considering. So what about *Godzilla*? I caught it on DVD last month."

"Seen the original?"

"No. What original?"

"Crikey, don't you know anything? It was first made in 1954 by the Japanese. Same thing applies. The Jap flick was an 'X,' the new one a PG, a kiddie's film."

"Yeah, I agree, it *was* slightly childish in places. Monster was good, though. You must have rated *King Kong*, surely."

"Yeah, OK, I enjoyed it, but there were too many dinosaurs, the pace was too frantic, and the music was non-existent. Max Steiner's score for the original is incredible—you *need* great music to complement what's going on, and you just don't have great music in fantasy pictures anymore. And have you noticed the color in the latest films? It's not exactly vibrant, is it?"

"What do you mean?"

"It seems flat, wishy-washy. Jan always reckons that the color in the older films was, well, more colorful, and she's right, it was. I've no idea why. They might have used new film stock, perhaps a lot of the modern-day movies are shot on videotape, I don't know. The old Hammer films are a prime example—beautiful, rich, inky color photography, especially in their earlier movies."

"Who's Hammer?"

Groan. "Bloody hell, Kenny, why don't you go and make a cup of tea or something."

"Well, who are they?"

"Never mind. I haven't got the time or the patience to explain."

"So you don't rate the new films then."

Sigh. "Look, they're not too bad for a night out but as soon as I leave the cinema, I forget about them, or most of them. None of them are memorable, I've seen so much forgettable crap recently: *House of Wax*, *The Day After Tomorrow*, *Van Helsing*, that musical version of *The Phantom of the Opera*, *The Core*, the first *Harry Potter* movie, *Vanilla Sky*, *Hollow Man*, *The Bunker*, *The Mummy Returns*..."

"You're off!"

"Yes, and you started it. Look, Kenny, I'm 59. You're 22. I've seen the classics—you didn't. I haven't got a lot of time for today's stuff. You're of a different generation, you obviously enjoy it, but it's not for me, well, most of it isn't, anyway."

"Have you always taken this matter so bloody seriously?"

The *War of the Worlds* remake featured high-tech aliens.

"Yes, I suppose I have, ever since I was a kid. And believe me, I drive Jan up the wall analyzing all the time, you know, the director should have done this, the music was too loud, that scene was badly done, the ending was rubbish—I've always been like it, particularly if a movie doesn't grab me. Me and my mates even used to compile our own little magazines with film reviews in them when I was at college, with lists of likes and dislikes. Sad, isn't it?"

"Not really—each to his own, that's what I always say. Tell you what, Barry, I'll have to come round your place one day and watch some of these so-called classics, see what I think of them."

"If you're in the market for a good old dose of black-and-white horror, be it monsters, Frankenstein, Dracula, giant insects, aliens—you name it, I've probably got it—then I'm your man."

"OK. Sounds interesting. How about next Sunday?"

"Whoa! Hang on. I'll have to check with the wife first. Perhaps I'll make a convert out of you yet!"

10

A CONVERSATION—THE OLD VERSUS THE NEW (2)

"Uncle Barry, next time you come over, can you bring some of your films with you."

"What films?"

"Some of your horror films."

"Yes, OK."

Two Months Later.

"Hi, Sue. Kids here?"

"Hi you two. Yes, they're in the spare room. Are we still on for shopping, Mum?"

"I reckon so. Baz can look after the boys, can't you, darling."

"Yep. No problem."

"What do you plan on doing to amuse them?"

"Show them those DVDs I brought over with us."

"What DVDs?"

"You know, the ones I picked up this morning."

"Not horror films, I hope."

"Well, a bit of horror, a bit of sci-fi and *Cesta Do Praveku*. I thought they'd enjoy that one, you're always telling me that Tom, Ollie, and Henry like dinosaurs."

"Never mind about *that* film. What about the others?"

"Well, do you remember that compilation DVD I did the other month, you know, when I spent nearly the whole of Sunday recording around 40 to 50 excerpts off tape onto disc?"

"You mean to tell me that with that famous analytical brain of yours, you don't know how many you actually recorded, and by that I mean the *exact* number."

"Don't be sarcastic Jan. It was 43."

"Yes, I do remember. Tapes cluttering the place up, much like your discs do now."

With a deep breath, then "Right. That's one of the DVDs. The other two are *Creature from the Black Lagoon* and *Gorgo*."

"You can't let them see those."

"Why not?"

"They'll be scared to death."

"Of course they won't. Luke watches them and he's only eight."

"Luke is your grandson, so he's probably inherited your traits, poor thing. Sue's lads are a bit more sensitive, aren't they, Sue."

"Well, Henry will get nightmares, Ollie might, but wouldn't admit to it, but, no, I don't think they would affect Tom. They're not all that bad, are they?"

"No, of course not. Look, Tom himself wanted me to bring them over the last time we were here so don't go blaming me."

Shrug, then "Well, I suppose it's alright just this once. Come on, Mum, let's be off and leave them to it."

"OK. We'll see you later. And Baz, don't go frightening those boys. I know what you're like."

"Don't worry. You two have fun. And don't spend too much."

"We won't."

Bang goes the front door, then "Hello you three. How you doing?"

"Hello Uncle Barry. We're fine thanks."

"I've brought those films over, Tom. Want to see them?"

"Yeah!" in unison.

"Right. We can see *Cesta Do Praveku* [*Journey to the Beginning of Time*] first, the one about the four boys going down the river and encountering all kinds of prehistoric life, that one I told you about on the phone, Tom. It's Czechoslovakian with French subtitles, so you can brush up on your French while it's on."

"OK."

Thirty minutes later.

"Uncle Barry, it's very slow, isn't it."

"Um, maybe. But the mammoth and other creatures are pretty good, don't you think."

"Well, not really, they look like little models, a bit jerky. When does it end?"

"Another hour yet. Hey, it *was* made in 1954, you know. And not with computers, either."

"How did they get the mammoth to work, then?"

"Right. Go back to that scene on the riverbank. That's it. The screen is split just along the waterline, and the mammoth on the bank is matted in after being filmed in stop-motion. That's when they move the model one fraction of an inch at a time and then film each movement one frame at a time. When the film is processed and run through a projector, you have established motion in the model. The boys are, in fact, looking at something else and the two separate pieces of film, that is the boys and the mammoth, are joined together. You've got to admit, it's a bloody, sorry, very clever piece of trick photography for the time it was made, don't you think?"

"Suppose so. But *Jurassic Park 3* was better. These old monsters look so corny."

Not a success, obviously. "Let's turn this off. Fancy *Gorgo*?"

"Yes!"

Eighty minutes and a couple of Cokes each later.

"Good?"

"Yeah." Thank God for that!

"Do you three realize that when *Gorgo* was shown at the cinema, it was an 'X' film, and now here you all are, 7, 11 and 12, watching it."

"What's an 'X' film?"

"Well, if a picture was an 'X,' it meant that you had to be 16 to watch it. Actually, I sneaked in to see it when I was about 14, as I did with a lot of other films, I can tell you."

"Was it hard to get in and see them?"

"It certainly was, Ollie, but I used to get away with it 'cos I was tall for my age at the time. Anyway, anyone for a biscuit and a drink?"

Fifteen minutes later.

"What's next. Do you want to see *Creature from the Black Lagoon* or this one where there are a lot of excerpts from different films?"

"The excerpts."

The excerpts or what we see of them prove to be a hit, as follows:

Gorgo (the monster storming the London streets): "Go forward, we've just seen that one."

It Conquered the World (the cucumber-shaped Venusian trundling out from its cave to confront the army): "Hah! We could make one of those things in school."

House of Dracula (Lon Chaney changing into the Wolf Man in the prison cell): "Cool!"

Doctor Blood's Coffin (the reactivated corpse attacking Kieron Moore): "Uncle Barry. Why is that man's face all green?" "He's dead—or he was."

The Beast from 20,000 Fathoms (the monster emerging near the docks): "That dinosaur is really good, isn't it Ollie." "Yes."

The Monster that Challenged the World (the giant caterpillar menacing Audrey Dalton and her daughter): "Henry. That thing's going to break into your bedroom tonight." "Tom. Shut up."

Tarantula (the spider clambering over the hillside as the townsfolk prepare to dynamite the road): "You can see that's not a real spider." "Actually, Ollie, it is, I think they used two in the film." "Oh."

The Mummy (Christopher Lee emerging from the swamp): "That's a pretty scary mummy, Henry, much better than the new one. Keep your door closed tonight." "Be quiet, you two."

The Black Scorpion (Denning's descent into the scorpions' lair): "Those monsters are really good. Bring the whole film over next time, I want to see how it ends."

The Fiend Who Walked the West (psycho Robert Evans and Hugh O'Brian's first encounter in prison): "Uncle Barry. What's a Western in here for?" "Because it was an 'X' certificate Western." "Why?" "I'll tell you later."

The Creature Walks Among Us (the gill-man running amok in Jeff Morrow's house): "Is that a man or something else. Where's he come from?"

The Thing from Another World (James Arness stalking Kenneth Tobey and company in the Quonset hut): "Is that an alien?" "Yep." "Er, he looks more like a human. What a rubbishy alien."

Blood Is My Heritage (Sandra Harrison turning into a vampire): "She's really creepy."

Godzilla (the original Toho monster trashing Tokyo): "Is that an old *Godzilla*?" "It's the 1954 version." "I thought *Godzilla* was a new film." "It was remade a few years ago." "The new one was better than this. You can't see what's going on, it's too dark."

The Curse of Frankenstein (Peter Cushing shoots Christopher Lee in the face): "Uncle Barry, why did he do that?" "Well, that monster was after him so he had to." "Where did the monster come from?" "He was made out of parts of dead bodies." "That's yuk."

Dracula (the first appearance of Christopher Lee in vampire-mode): "Wow! Look at him."

King Kong (Kong breaking out of the theater): "Uncle Barry. Can you bring that one over too."

From Hell It Came (the perambulating tree stump on the prowl): "Tom. I think that's a man in a rubber suit." "Yes, I know, stupid."

Day the World Ended (the mutant menacing Richard Denning and Lori Nelson): "Uncle Barry, why's that man got three eyes and funny little arms on his shoulders?" "He's suffered from atomic radiation, and he's not really a man. He's a mutant." "Don't look at him, Henry." Silence from Henry.

Alien (the chest-bursting sequence): "That's cool, isn't it Henry." Silence from Henry.

The Amazing Colossal Man (60-foot-high Glenn Langan strolling through Las Vegas): "That's crap. Look, you can see right through him."

Earth vs. the Flying Saucers (Harryhausen's saucers invading Washington): "Uncle Barry. Those flying saucers aren't as good as the ones in *Independence Day*." Deep, audible sigh. "That's a matter of opinion, Tom."

The Quatermass Experiment (the chemist uncovering Richard Wordsworth's infected arm): "Ugh! Look at his arm. Uncle Barry, is he an alien?" "No, not quite."

House of Wax (Vincent Price pursuing Phyllis Kirk through the misty streets): "I don't like his face." "I don't think you should see any more of this, Henry." "I'm going to."

Them! (the huge ants lurching over a sand dune): "Are they real ants magnified?" "No, very large models." "Hmmm. They look really great."

The Seventh Voyage of Sinbad (the first appearance of the Cyclops): "Cool. Greek mythology, Uncle Barry?" "No, Arabian Nights, Tom."

"Hi, you lot. We're home. What are you watching?" (just as werewolf Matt Willis in *The Return of the Vampire* lopes across the screen). "Baz, turn that off, now."

"But they're lapping it up."

"Yes, Granny, we are."

"No, that's your lot. Sue?"

"Yes, come on. Dinner's ready in a few minutes anyway."

After dinner.

"So, you three, what do you think of Uncle Barry's films?"

"Well, some of them are alright, but others are a bit boring. Why aren't they *all* in color?"

"Color doesn't necessarily make a good film, Tom."

"Don't start expounding your theories and ideas on what makes a good film to him, Barry. He's too young to be putting up with all of that. Just accept the fact that the kids these days like something a bit brighter and flashier than those antiques you're always glued to."

"Thanks. Don't I know it."

"What did they get to see, then?"

"Well, some of those excerpts."

"How many of those excerpts, exactly?"

"Um, about 20 snippets on the compilation, maybe a bit more, the whole of *Gorgo*, part of *Journey to the Beginning of Time* (*Cesta do praveku*, 1955), which for some funny reason they didn't think much of, and we haven't got around to the *Creature* movie yet."

Journey to the Beginning of Time **wasn't a hit with my younger viewers.**

"And you're not going to. That's enough for them today. I just hope your little afternoon's entertainment doesn't give them sleepless nights."

"It won't. Crikey, those pictures are years old. Sue's boys didn't bat an eyelid when they were watching them. The computer games they play with are a thousand times worse and they don't get nightmares from those."

"Well, they had better not, that's all I'm saying."

A week later.

"Sue rang me at work today."

"Yeah?"

"Yes. She's had trouble with Ollie and particularly Henry. Henry's been wandering into her bed in the middle of the night, crying, saying he can't sleep, and Ollie's been trying to put off going to bed. In fact, he wanted to sleep in Tom's room the other night."

"Why?"

"You damn well know why, Baz. Those blasted film clips you showed them, that's why. Henry was moaning things like nasty faces and monsters, Ollie's

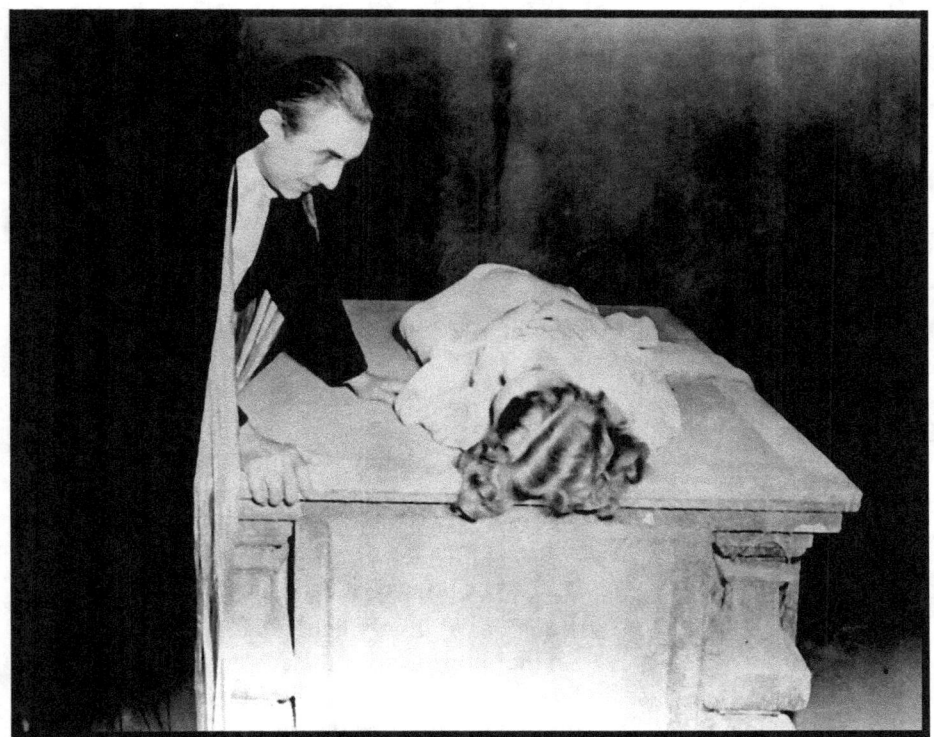
Bela Lugosi in *Return of the Vampire* is much scarier than Freddy or Jason!

gone very quiet and now Sue is lumbered with the job of sorting them out until they forget about what they saw."

"How about Tom?"

"Never mind about Tom, he's OK, he's older than Ollie and Henry. I *knew* you shouldn't have taken those DVDs over."

"Well, at least it serves to illustrate a point."

"Which is?"

"That kids today as young as Tom, Ollie, and Henry can sit through all of these "18" certified nasty videos and I know they've seen "18" certificate movies as well. Tom let slip that they had, but the oldies still possess the capability to put fear in them, however many years ago they were made."

"So you did it as an experiment, then."

"No, just to add three more converts to the cause. But as I said, they really did enjoy them."

"I'll pass judgment on that. Don't go trying to convert any more kids to your so-called cause. *You* may have this ongoing fascination with old black-and-white horror films, others may not share that fascination, whether you like it or not."

"Yes, chicken. Put the kettle on, will you?"

11

POSTSCRIPT

In *You're Not Old Enough Son*, I rounded off the first part of the book with my observations on what I had seen from 1954 to 1970. The films that had made an impression, those that hadn't, favorite scenes, great soundtracks, memorable double bills, not so memorable double bills, beguiling posters, unforgettable lines of dialogue, underrated flicks, and overrated flicks. Rounding off this book with similar observations is difficult. 1954 to 1970 were the glory years, which is something one could never say about the 34 years that followed. Classics abounded during that golden period of cinema-going, which I documented in my first book. They are very few and far between in the decades that came after. To be truthful, hardly any stick in the memory or have retained that magic ingredient called lasting power. *Alien* perhaps. Maybe *A Clockwork Orange* and *The Elephant Man*. Possibly *Star Wars* if you are into that kind of thing, but little else. A hotchpotch of differing styles combined with the disposable culture we now find ourselves in means that movies and in particular, that undervalued sector of the cinema called fantasy, do not carry that much weight nowadays. See it once or don't bother—it'll be in the shops soon is the current way of thinking. Film, like everything else in the 21st century, is also fast becoming disposable. The days when a relatively low-budget sci-fi thriller such as *20 Million Miles*

The Mad Ghoul

to Earth played on the circuits for 10 years and entertained God-knows how many packed houses during that time are but a distant memory. The public just isn't interested anymore in paying money to see movies time and time again in a cinema. As a consequence, this, in my view, has spelt the end of the classic HSFF film. Younger folk may not agree with these sentiments, but *they* never sat in a cinema and witnessed Willis O'Brien's giant animated scorpion clambering over Mexico City's bullring to do battle with the military in *The Black Scorpion,* or squirmed in terror as maniacal John Beal loped through the streets in *The Vampire. They* were never enthralled at the sight of a rampaging *Kronos* stomping all over the countryside firing off bolts of lightning, or edged further back into their seats as wild-eyed zombie David Bruce approached nearer and nearer to the camera in *The Mad Ghoul,* or were gobsmacked at the sight of Jack Arnold's *Tarantula* tearing up the house from which it had escaped. *They* never shivered in fear as the fiery medieval devil from hell materialized in the opening minutes of *Night of the Demon,* or gaped in awe when *Varan the Unbelievable* reduced a native village to rubble, or felt the hairs rising on their arms as Alberto Lupo transformed himself into *Seddok, Son of Satan. They* never jumped several inches out of their seats as the lock-keeper was dispatched by *The Monster that Challenged the World* or sniggered in derision when the puppet-like giant spider trotted onto the set of *Missile to the Moon*. These were enduring images, each and every one of them. They simply do not exist in modern-day HSFF fare. So, as I have stated, it has been hard to come up with a top 20 list of this and that for the newer fare, but after a great deal of rummaging around, I've managed the following, giving them, as us fantasy buffs are wont to do (and love to do), ratings out of five as below:

*****   A modern-day classic
****   Excellent, containing high production values
***   Good, entertaining enough with a touch of class
**   Average, some worthwhile points to recommend it
*   Poor, deficient in every department and unattractive to view

Worth the price of a ticket (The Very Good)

Alien—The 1950s brand of sci-fi given a big-budget treatment, a tension-fueled chiller featuring one of the genre's most arresting and formidable space monsters. Despite the array of expensive hardware on display, the '50s lived on in one of the few modern-day classics of its kind. *****

Batman—An intelligent opening for the Caped Crusader franchise, Michael Keaton bringing a welcome air of gravitas to the dual role of Bruce Wayne/Batman, pitted against Jack Nicholson's fiendishly over-the-top Joker in a tainted and corrupt Gotham City. ****

A Clockwork Orange—Kubrick's notorious vision of a violent future, with Malcolm McDowell's thuggish Alex one of the screen's most beguiling anti-heroes. The helter-skelter pace of the first half more than compensates for lapses in the final 50 minutes and it still remains a never-repeated moment in cinema history. *****

Contact—Astronomer Jodie Foster makes contact with a mysterious alien coded message, taking her on an unfathomable odyssey into the unknown. This is intelligent fare for the discerning buff. ****

The Descent—A shocking fate awaits six women, who venture into an unknown system of caves inhabited by hordes of ravenous and revolting beasts. Bloody, horrific, dynamic, and, in the final moments, quite moving. ****

Donnie Darko—A disturbed youth experiences flashbacks and odd events related to a terrible accident in which he may or may not have perished. This is a real puzzle of a film, which ultimately could have several different endings depending on the imaginative powers of each individual watching it. ****

Ed Wood—Tim Burton's affectionate tribute to the King of the Awful, Edward D. Wood Junior, is beautifully shot in monochrome with Martin Landau outstanding as a cantankerous Bela Lugosi in his final days. *****

Alien was worth the price of admission.

The Elephant Man—An immensely heart-rending telling of the story of sideshow freak John Merrick, his fight to survive in Victorian London, and his friendship with a surgeon played by Anthony Hopkins. It is finely photographed in gritty black and white by veteran cameraman Freddie Francis. *****

The Empire Strikes Back—The best of the original *Star Wars* trilogy. It is energetic, has terrific effects, and has a more lucid script than its predecessor. Harrison Ford also shines as rogue hero Han Solo. ****

The Fly—The 1958 kitsch horror classic upgraded to include graphically gruesome transmutation scenes and a winning performance from Jeff Goldblum in the title role. ****

Frankenstein and the Monster from Hell—The last of Hammer's long run of *Frankenstein* pictures is a rather cold and detached entry in the series, reuniting Peter Cushing, Terence Fisher, and composer James Bernard. The result is a return to form for Britain's once-famous purveyors of top-class horror. ****

High Plains Drifter—The avenging spirit of cowpoke Clint Eastwood exacts violent retribution on the town that put him to death in a highly stylized fantasy Western directed with finesse by the star himself. ****

Jurassic Park 3—Monster mayhem a la the 1950s—short and snappy, the personable Sam Neill carrying the day and a nice selection of monsters, which don't overstay their welcome. ****

King Kong—Okay, it is *not* in the same league as RKO's venerable classic, but let's all give director Peter Jackson at least four stars out of five for blowing $200 million on his pet project, endeavoring to present to a jaded cinema-going public a remake that would lift their imaginative spirits to an all-time high as the first *Kong* had done all those years ago. In the DVD-obsessed society of 2005, it wasn't the colossal success the backers had hoped for, but regardless of its lack of pull at the box office, *King Kong* is a good-enough example of modern filmmaking. ****

Lord of the Rings: The Two Towers—Three hours of epic battles, intricate plotting, a devious Gollum, breathtaking backdrops, walking trees, and outlandish monsters, none of which makes a great deal of sense to non-*Lord of the Rings* devotees such as myself, but is enjoyable anyway. ****

The Others—A genuine edge-of-the-seat spine-chiller of the type they rarely make these days. It is relatively low budget, has minimal effects, and a small cast acting their socks off in a superior haunted house drama with a deeply tragic ending. ****

Pitch Black—A space crew run for their lives when a distant planet they are marooned on is plunged into darkness following a duel eclipse, the signal for swarms of voracious airborne aliens to attack them in their thousands. Vin Diesel as the villain turned goodie kept the momentum going in a relentless and old-fashioned sci-fi action flick that proved to be an unexpected hit in the United Kingdom. ****

Predator—Arnold and his group of commandos are dropped into the Central American jungle on a mission and soon find themselves combating an alien big-game hunter, who is more than a match for them. A witty script, authentic jungle locations, and an unconventional space creature all contributed to a highly enjoyable slice of late-'80s slam-bang hokum. ****

Starship Troopers—Space cadets fresh from academy clash with an army of gigantic insects on the planet Klendathu in Paul Verhoeven's lively and grisly take on dozens of '50s sci-fi bug movies. ****

The Thing—John Carpenter's retread of Howard Hawks' pioneering sci-fi thriller goes all out for repulsive effects and sags in the middle section, but still comes across as a weighty piece of X-rated other-worldly horror, viewed in a far more favorable light now by fans than when it was first released. ****

Well, that was OK, wasn't it? (The Not-So-Bad)

An American Werewolf in London—Landmark transformation scenes, wicked humor, and attractive leads lift this latter-day werewolf movie out of the rut into the minor classic league. ****

Capricorn One—Three astronauts find their lives are in danger when threatening to expose a faked Mars mission. It is scattered, uneven in mood, has erratic direction, but nonetheless captivating in a corny kind of way. ***

Cronos—A Mexican-produced oddity concerning an intricate device that can bestow upon its owner the power of eternal life, but at a bloodthirsty cost. Little seen in England, this was a different take on the old vampire myth, put across with verve and style. ***

Edward Scissorhands—A fairy tale for adults, Tim Burton placing his *Frankenstein*-type creation in the pastel suburbs only to be cast back into the castle from whence he came. Johnny Depp excels as the shear-handed waif misunderstood by the townsfolk. ***

The Exorcist—Vomiting, obscenities, hideous makeup, and hammy histrionics on a grand scale as possessed Linda Blair proves to be a real handful for priest Max von Sydow in one of the '70s biggest box office hits. ****

From Hell—Jack the Ripper revisited in a far gorier fashion than before, an underrated horror flick starring Johnny Depp as the detective on the killer's trail in a grimly portrayed East End of London. Not for the faint-hearted! ***

The Funhouse—A bunch of frisky teenagers decide to spend the night in a carnival funhouse and are picked off by a murderous freak lurking within the

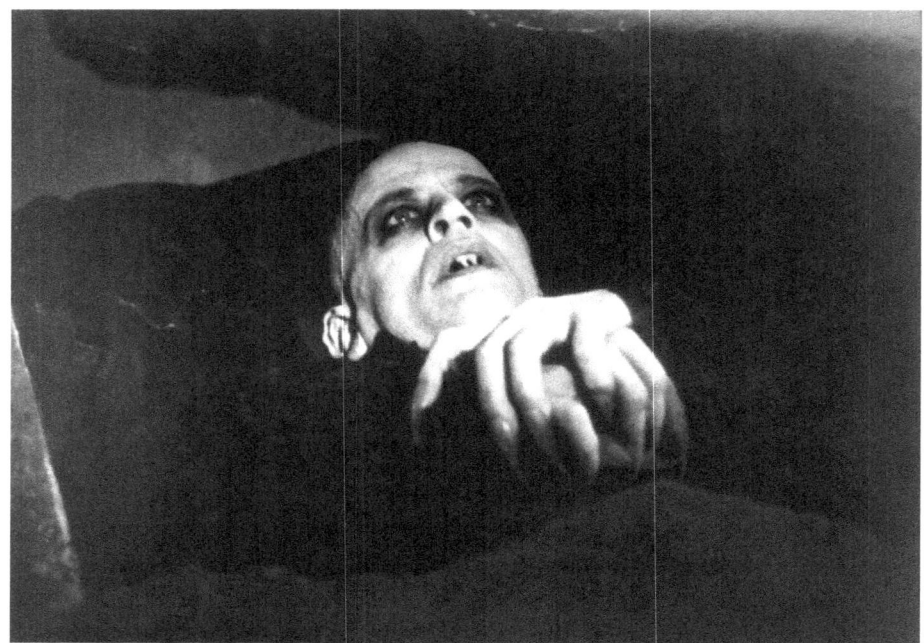

Klaus Kinski in *Nosferatu the Vampyre*

exhibits. This is an early teen horror movie, where Tobe Hooper manipulates his cast with relish. ***

Ghost Ship—A salvage crew board a derelict liner and encounter the evil spirits of the passengers, who perished there years before. It's well-paced 18-rated horror fodder with a neat twist in the tail. ***

Gods and Monsters—James Whale's infatuation with his gardener during the making of *Bride of Frankenstein* was the theme of this haunting tribute to one of the genre's earliest exponents of classic horror. ***

Logan's Run—Garish '70s comic strip fantasy with a fine second half set in a desolate and weed-encrusted Washington as escapees Michael York and Jenny Agutter meet kindly old sage Peter Ustinov. ***

Mighty Joe Young—Disney overhauls the old RKO-Radio giant ape thriller, where the outcome reveals some eye-catching CGI effects and a credible monster for a change. ***

The Ninth Gate—Johnny Depp yet again, an unscrupulous dealer on the hunt for a notorious book on the black arts that holds the secret to the gates of hell. Roman Polanski's mystical chiller, unfairly admonished by the critics, was a rewarding excursion into the realms of the supernatural and was carefully paced and well-acted. ****

Nosferatu the Vampyre—Klaus Kinski takes on the Max Schreck role as the talon and dome-headed bloodsucker in a rather plodding remake that nevertheless contains some creepy sequences worthy of the 1922 original. ***

Picnic at Hanging Rock—Peter Weir's enigmatic and art-house movie concerning the mysterious disappearance of a group of schoolgirls in the Australian outback went against the violent grain of mid-1970s cinema and emerged a winner. ***

Sinbad and the Eye of the Tiger—Ray Harryhausen, against all the odds, carried on with his unique brand of fantasy and this particular *Sinbad* proved to be an oddly endearing little movie, despite lapses in plot development and some pretty ropy trick work towards the end. ***

Solaris—Russia's reply to *2001: A Space Odyssey* challenged the mind and the senses. The masses ignored it, but die-hard sci-fi fans savored the movie to the full. ****

Star Trek IV: The Voyage Home—At long last, Paramount managed, after three attempts, to capture the essence of the television series in this highly entertaining and great-looking science fiction blockbuster featuring all of our favorites in peak form. ****

Susperia—The continental horror/splatter movie is alive and well in Dario Argento's blood-soaked frightener concerning a reactivated witch in a girls' dancing academy. ****

Tales from the Crypt—Amicus produced a number of horror compilations and this, their third, was one of their worthier efforts, with a great British cast (including Peter Cushing) doing justice to the horror writings of William Gaines. ***

Time After Time—Jack the Ripper steals H.G. Wells' time machine, ending up in San Francisco where he continues his nefarious deeds. It's a fine pairing of David Warner and Malcolm McDowell together with a rousing score that contributes to a much-underrated fantasy/horror picture. ***

Can I have a refund, please? (The Downright Ugly)

Alien 3—Unsympathetic characters, continuous swearing, murky photography, and a little-seen monster do not make a good sci-fi movie. *

Audrey Rose—A turgid and talkative reincarnation melodrama that most people I knew lost interest in halfway through the picture. **

The Bunker—*The Clunker* would have been a more apt description of this cut-price British effort, which showed how bad us Brits could be sometimes in trying to produce top-notch horror, which this wasn't. *

Demolition Man—A big and dumb coarse example of modern-day sci-fi fare, suitable for Sylvester Stallone perhaps, but not for the audience watching it. **

Dracula AD 1972—The worst of the Hammer *Dracula* flicks, the flare and imagination that used to be the company's trademark nowhere in evidence, with Cushing and Lee simply going through the motions. **

The Ghoul—Despite Freddie Francis in the director's seat, this substandard Hammer-type effort is lackluster in all departments, the monster of the title simply a cannibalistic son in a loin cloth locked in the attic. Even Peter Cushing looked uncomfortable in it. *

Hannibal—A boring and very long sequel to *The Silence of the Lambs*. If you are fascinated by the exploits of Hannibal Lecter, by all means see it. If not, don't bother. **

The Haunting—An exercise in how *not* to make a hair-raising supernatural haunted house chiller. A riot of over-the-top effects to appease the kids (filmed in daylight and not at night) and the "12" rating says it all. *

The Incredible Melting Man—William Sachs attempts a '70s version of a '50s B movie and falls flat on his face. Compare this to 1959's *First Man into Space* and you'll see what I mean. *

Independence Day—Over-inflated alien invasion blockbuster hampered by a trite script, the impressive (to begin with) visuals not compensating for a complete lack of dramatics or character development, a multimillion-dollar video game pandering to the juveniles, and not to those who hold the genre in high regard. **

King Kong—RKO's 1933 classic reduced to Jessica Lange sucking up to a man in a gorilla suit. Even Toho's Kong, which featured in some of their '60s monster movies, was a more powerful figure than this one. **

Lost in Space—We all loved the 1960s TV series, second only to *Star Trek* in genuine authenticity, but charming all the same. Most buffs loathed the cinema version, a high velocity, very noisy, and utterly disagreeable update that bombed at the box office, thus preventing the makers from inflicting a sequel onto the public, as was mooted at one point. *

The Lost World: Jurassic Park—Spielberg's expensive no-brainer of a sequel to *Jurassic Park* ranks as one of the most infantile dinosaur movies ever made. Even Fairview's 1960 *Dinosaurus!* had more going for it. Jeff Goldblum's pained and miserable expression summed up perfectly the feelings of the audience! *

The Mask—If you're a Jim Carrey fan, then this is fine. If not, this geek-turned-superhero effort will turn your stomach as the star mugs his way through a series of cartoon escapades, the delectable Cameron Diaz the only reason for non-Carrey aficionados to watch. *

Meteor—A trashy '70s disaster movie throwing all characterization and plot out of the window in exchange for a welter of unconvincing effects, rotten color photography, and a tired script. *

The Mummy—1932—the Karloff classic; 1959—the Christopher Lee classic; 1999—the Brendan Fraser bummer. **

Psycho—Hitchcock must have been revolving in his grave at the very thought of someone else tampering with his masterpiece. It's just as well that he wasn't around to witness Gus Van Sant's misconceived interference with the genre's key psychological horror thriller, which served no useful purpose other than to reinforce the significance of the 1960 original. *

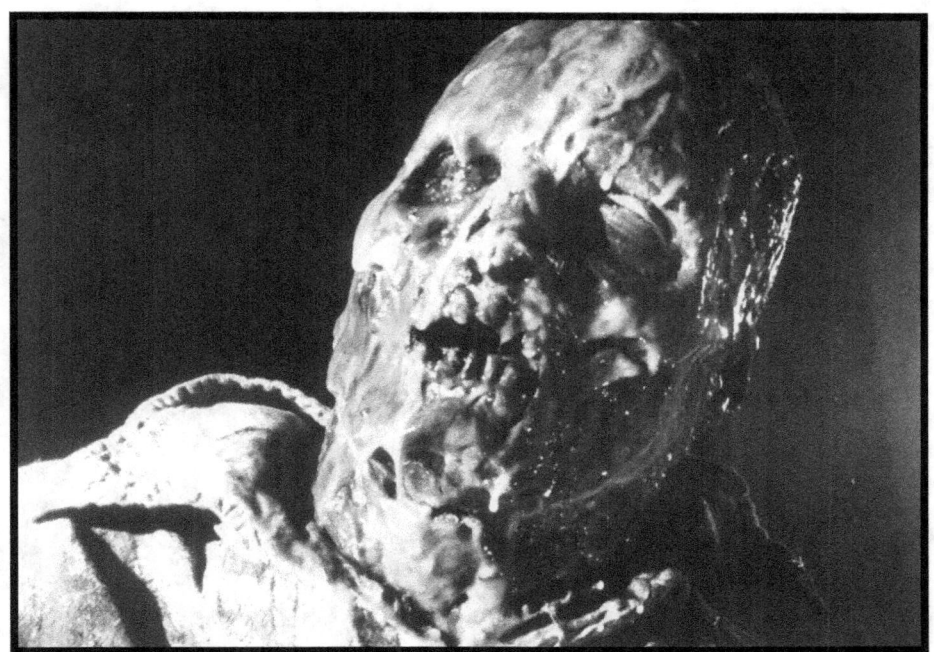

The Incredible Melting Man melted, but wasn't that incredible.

Total Recall—Paul Verhoeven's ham-fisted, confusing tale of a conspiracy on Mars, complete with explosions, endless fights, and a deadpan Schwarzenegger mouthing witless one-liners, makes for deeply unattractive viewing. **

Van Helsing—The golden years of Universal's *Frankenstein*, *Dracula,* and *Mummy* pictures simply did not deserve this horrendous parody of the genre. Lifelong fans of HSFF, along with most critics, gave it the thumbs down. It's getting only one star in my book for this perversion. *

X-Men—Empty-headed superhero shenanigans, all done before, each movie trying desperately to come up with something different, all culminating in the villain being defeated, a yawn-inducing indictment of current-day trends in fantasy cinema and how far downhill most of it has traveled. **

Major disappointments
(You could have done a lot better here, Mister Director)

A.I.—Artificial Intelligence—Spielberg should have left out the brash middle section in android city and put his directorial powers to better use on the beginning and the end to create a more cohesive sci-fi fable. **

The Blair Witch Project—Horror for the camcorder generation, most of the footage in the second half consisting of a leafy woodland floor. A scary scenario ruined by amateur dramatics. **

The Golden Voyage of Sinbad failed to live up to the previous efforts.

Bram Stoker's Dracula—The Gothic mood conjured up in the opening 30 minutes was not sustained by Francis Ford Coppola for the remainder of the film, which relied too much on up-to-date gruesome transformation scenes to satisfy the new audience, but not old lags such as myself. ***

Close Encounters of the Third Kind—Highfaluting sci-fi of the boring kind, the director redeeming himself with the much-improved special edition in 1980. ***

The Fifth Element—Yet another in the cycle of promising beginning, but shame about the rest of it, a brand of expensive science fantasy that had serious critics tearing their hair out in despair because of what *might* have been. **

The Golden Voyage of Sinbad—Gordon Hessler's uninspired and heavy-footed fantasy disappointed because the movie, despite Harryhausen's effects, failed to live up to Columbia's pre-1970 output, which it should have taken more heed of. **

Jurassic Park—The dinosaurs were OK (for the time), but Spielberg might have paid a little more attention to plot development, characterization, and a decent script. Ditching those kids would have helped as well. **

Lifeforce—A fantastic opening few minutes set in space plummets into nonsense as Tobe Hooper's sci-fi/horror goes completely off the rails for reasons best known only to himself. *

Mary Shelley's Frankenstein—Kenneth Branagh went all worthy on us and came up with one of the dullest versions of Mary Shelley's novel ever made. **

The Omen—One over-staged ghastly death after another plus a distinctly non-scary Damien added up to a big and flashy dose of theatrics containing less edge-of-the-seat suspense than the average Hammer horror movie. **

The Phantom of the Opera—Years in the making and protracted arguments over who should star and what happens? It's an expensive flop with Andrew Lloyd Webber's magnificent music hindered by stagy production values and non-memorable leading players. **

Poltergeist—Tobe Hooper and Steven Spielberg preoccupied themselves with cramming too many monstrosities into the movie's running time. The end result is tedium on a massive scale. It's a movie about paranormal activity that backfired on the let's scare the audience front. **

The Satanic Rites of Dracula—Why couldn't Hammer have enlisted the services of Terence Fisher and James Bernard (as in *Frankenstein and the Monster from Hell*) to ensure that their final *Dracula* outing was a blinder, and not, as it turned out, a stinker. **

The Shining—Stephen King's bone-chilling haunted house novel received the Stanley Kubrick treatment and contained some spooky moments, but more or less gave in to showing the public what a maniacal actor Jack Nicholson could be if given material such as this to work on. ***

Signs—M. Night Shyamalan's sci-fi drama moved at the pace of a snail with migraine towards its not unexpected conclusion. Even cheap films such as *The Cosmic Man* (1958) were quicker than this! **

Silent Running—I'm all for a film coming in at under two hours, but 89 minutes for an ambitious picture of this sort is short-changing the punter. Splendid visuals failed to compensate for a complete lack of thrills, an omen of what was to follow in the 1970s. ***

Species—A heavily edited, incoherent sci-fi/horror featuring some diabolical stop-motion trickery, Giger's *Alien*-type she-monster was the victim of the cutting room floor even though the movie was 18-rated. **

Star Trek: The Motion Picture—The long-awaited big-screen version of the revered TV series should have been shorter and snappier, not 132 monotonous minutes that tested the stamina of even the most seasoned Trekker. **

Star Wars—Adult science fiction fantasy makes way for juvenilia on a hyped-up level never encountered before. It's an empty spectacle for the kids to spend their money on and for long-standing disciples of fantasy to mourn for the days of *This Island Earth*. ***

Wolfen—A detective thriller passing itself off as a horror film. Large wolves, like bees do not make for horrifying viewing, however well-made the product is. **

Too good for television—they should have been unleashed at the cinema

The Night Stalker—Newshound Carl Kolchak ignores police warnings and tracks down a vampire in modern-day Las Vegas. It's rollicking fun with Darren McGavin in top form as the kooky reporter with a knack for rubbing everybody the wrong way. ***

The Night Strangler—Superior to *The Night Stalker*, *Strangler* sees Kolchak uncovering a sinister secret in the bowels of Seattle's underground city involving a century-old alchemist with a thirst for human blood. ****

The Norliss Tapes—Enterprising sub-Kolchak special with Roy Thinnes as the investigative reporter this time, tracking down a devil-type being, who is behind a series of slayings. ***

Quatermass—Not in the same league as Nigel Kneale's fabulous *Quatermass* '50s trilogy, but a three-hour edit of the four-hour serial would have done well on the circuits, ideally introducing the Professor to a new generation of cinemagoers. ***

Salem's Lot—Top marks for the Number One adaptation of a Stephen King book, a mesmerizing, nerve-racking, and intricately plotted vampire chiller, which should be seen in its entire three-hour version. Regrettably, it never made it onto the big screen, a real pity as this is high-quality horror fare all round. *****

The Stone Tape—Dated, perhaps, but Nigel Kneale's tale of a hidden basement haunted by centuries-old specters would make an ideal vehicle for a modern-day supernatural picture if handled properly. ****

Threads—BBC's devastating prophecy of the effects of nuclear war in England shocked the public at the time and, because of its disturbing content, has not been broadcast since. ****

Double bills no longer exist in England's cinemas and since 1971, only a handful of such programs have grabbed my imagination. Unfortunately, none have really rivaled the listings in my previous book, where I was spoilt for choice when compiling a selection of 20 favorites, having, without any exaggeration whatsoever, scores to choose from. So scratching around, all I've been able to come up with is a top 12 list, which wasn't easy in itself:

Freaks and *Island of Lost Souls*
Alien and *The Fog*
Tales from the Crypt and *From Beyond the Grave*
Creature from the Black Lagoon and *It Came from Outer Space*
The Abominable Dr. Phibes and *Dr. Phibes Rises Again*
Altered States and *It Lives Again*
The Funhouse and *My Bloody Valentine*
Candyman and *Cronos*

Legend of the Werewolf and *Vampire Circus*
Hands of the Ripper and *Twins of Evil*
Halloween and *House of Whipcord*
Asylum and *Duel*

Sadly, apart from the odd soundtrack (*Alien, Susperia, Jaws, A Clockwork Orange*), memorable movie scores have been, and still are, thin on the ground, ear-shattering distinctly non-melodic noise replacing the symphonic tones of Bernard Herrmann and his kind. The music, when not blasting out, burbles along ineffectively in the background (quite often a non-stop tinkling piano and nothing else), a pop song bearing no relation to the motion picture one has just sat through often plays over the end credits—definitely no top-20 list here, then. Notable scenes, though, do crop up from time to time. This, I will happily admit. The following are 20 splendid moments that made me sit up and concentrate instead of panning what was in front of me. A sign, possibly, that the genre continues (although struggles) to survive, albeit in a different guise and with less significance than that of yesteryear:

Alien—The three astronauts exploring the ghostly and derelict alien ship on the bleak and storm-racked planetoid discover the fossilized pilot, an unsettling sequence underlined by Jerry Goldsmith's haunting score.

Bram Stoker's Dracula—Gary Oldman's Dracula gliding across the room towards Jonathan Harker, his flickering shadow playing tricks of its own on the candle-lit walls.

Clash of the Titans—Perseus squaring up to Medusa, the snake-headed Gorgon, on the Isle of the Dead, reveals a telling fusion of Harryhausen's dynamic effects within a nightmare setting.

A Clockwork Orange—The opening footage, Kubrick's camera slowly drawing back from an unblinking, smirking, and glammed-up Malcolm McDowell and his droogs backed by the droning electronic music of Walter Carlos, a splendid scene-setter for the mayhem to follow.

Contact—The mystifying closing 20 minutes as Jodie Foster undertakes a journey to discover the source of an alien signal, finding herself in a perplexing and parallel universe where everything is not what it seems.

Ed Wood—Martin Landau, spellbinding as an aging and drug-addicted Bela Lugosi, sitting in his gloomy lodgings, reliving past glories on his television set.

The Elephant Man—The moving climax whereby John Hurt decides to lay on his bed as normal people do to sleep, thus precipitating his own death.

Final Destination 2—The vehicle pile-up at the beginning, a heart-stopping shot, and with enough carnage on display to make any driver hesitate when getting behind the wheel of a car.

Godzilla—Godzilla erupts into sight from beneath the New York streets in front of a terrified Matthew Broderick.

Jurassic Park—Tyrannosaurus Rex crashes through the compound barrier—CGI has arrived. A few magical moments in an otherwise derivative picture that took the breath away, even from veterans of hundreds of monster flicks, including myself.

King Kong (2005)—Kong's final stand atop the giddy heights of the Empire State building, Peter Jackson orchestrating his zooming camerawork to perfection, ensuring that there won't be a dry eye in the house after the fatal climax.
Logan's Run—Michael York and Jenny Agutter wandering through a vegetation-encrusted, ruined Washington, an oddly evocative sequence somewhat out of step in a gaudy and flashy production.
Lord of the Rings: The Two Towers—The awesome Battle of Helm's Deep. Good versus Evil on an epic scale courtesy of CGI.
The Others—The heart-rending closing minutes as Nicole Kidman stumbles upon a séance and realizes that the ghosts that she and her children have been encountering are in fact the living—she and her children are the ghosts.
Q, The Winged Serpent—The giant flying reptile attacking the military at the top of New York's Chrysler Building, where it has built its nest, reminiscent in many ways of a 1950s Japanese monster flick and none the worse for it.
Raiders of the Lost Ark—Supernatural retribution as the Nazis open the Ark of the Covenant to reveal nothing, but dust—and then the avenging wraiths appear!

Sinbad and the Eye of the Tiger—The first appearance of the Troglodyte, one of Ray Harryhausen's most appealing latter-day creations.
Starship Troopers—An army of giant and mandible-waving bugs attacking the troops on the desolate planet of Klendathu.
Star Trek IV: The Voyage Home—Spock silencing a noisy yobbo on a San Francisco bus by administrating the Vulcan hand grip.
The Thing—The sequence in the kennels as the Husky reveals itself to be the alien of the title, a grisly transformation scene guaranteed to upset even the strongest of stomachs.

As far as noteworthy snippets of dialogue are concerned, these have traveled down the same route as the soundtrack—nothing really sticks in the mind. The older classics were chock-a-block with quirky, cranky, and witty lines, whereby many were unintentionally (or intentionally) hilarious (RKO's *King Kong*, for instance, is full to the brim with wonderful samples of interchange). The newer movies are by and large bereft of these scintillating gems from the scriptwriters' pens. Avoiding the obvious (*Jaws*: "We're gonna need a bigger boat." *Terminator 2*: "Hasta la Vista, Baby." *The Shining*: "Here's Johnny!" *Star Wars*: "May the Force Be With You."), here are a dozen fairly amusing examples of the scriptwriters' art which I've scraped together:

Alien
Yaphet Kotto to the crew: "This son of a bitch is huge! I mean, it's like a man—it's big!"

Batman
Jack Nicholson as the Joker: "Batman! Batman! Can somebody tell me what kind of a world we live in where a man dressed up as a bat gets all of my press? This town needs an enemy."

Capricorn One
James Brolin to Hal Holbrook on seeing the mock-up studio Martian landing for the first time: "You don't really think you're going to get away with this, do you?"

A Clockwork Orange
Malcom McDowell's voice-over as the film commences: "There was me, that is Alex, and my three droogs, that is Pete, Georgie and Dim, and we sat in the Korova milk bar trying to make up our rassoodocks what to do with the evening. The Korova milk bar sold milk-plus that is milk plus vellocet, or synthemesc, or drencrom which was what we were drinking. This would sharpen you up and get you ready for a bit of the old ultra-violence."

Ed Wood
Studio technician: "You know which movie of yours I love, Mr. Lugosi. *The Invisible Ray*. You were great as Karloff's sidekick."

Jack Nicholson as The Joker in *Batman*

Martin Landau: "Karloff? Sidekick? Fuck you! Karloff does not deserve to smell my shit! That limey cocksucker can rot in hell for all I care."

The Elephant Man
Anne Bancroft: "Oh, Mr. Merrick. You're not an Elephant Man at all."
John Hurt. "No?"
Anne Bancroft: "No. You're Romeo."

The Fly
Jeff Goldblum: "I know what the disease wants."
Geena Davis: "What does the disease want?"
Jeff Goldblum: "It wants to turn me into something else. That's not too terrible, is it? Most people will give anything to be turned into something else."
Geena Davis: "Turn into what?"
Jeff Goldblum: "What d'ya think. A fly? I'm becoming a 185-pound fly. No such thing has ever existed before. I'm becoming Brundle-fly. Don't you think that's worth a Nobel Prize or two?"

Frankenstein and the Monster from Hell
Shane Briant to the horrified policeman, who has just dropped a jar full of eyeballs onto the lab floor: "You bloody fool. If you could only appreciate the difficulty in finding specimens like these."

High Plains Drifter
Cowboy to Clint Eastwood: "Flea-bitten range bums don't usually stop in Lago. Life here is a little too quick for 'em. Maybe you think you're fast enough to keep up with us, huh?"
Clint Eastwood: "I'm faster than you'll ever live to be."
Predator
Schwarzenegger, staring up as the alien removes his helmet: "You're one ugly motherfucker!"
Star Trek IV: The Voyage Home
Catherine Hicks: "Who are you?"
William Shatner: "Who do you think I am?"
Catherine Hicks: "Don't tell me. You're from Outer Space."
William Shatner: "No, I'm from Iowa. I only work in Outer Space."
The Thing
Richard Masur to Kurt Russell as the alien-dog reveals itself: "I don't know what the hell's in there, but it's weird and pissed off, whatever it is."

This book draws to a conclusion at the very end of 2005—over 50 years of fantasy cinema under my belt and it still continues to this day. Already in 2006, I've taken in *The Hills Have Eyes*, superior to the 1977 original, a high-class horror movie that has pace, tremendous desert locations, a race of hideous mutants, and buckets of blood, *Children of Men*, a depressingly realistic vision

Lord of the Rings: Galadriel (Cate Blanchett) tells Frodo (Elijah Wood) goodbye.

of a lawless England in the future where all women are infertile, and *Hostel*, also with loads of blood and guts, but little else to recommend it. Oh yes, plus a second trip to Peter Jackson's *King Kong* before it vanishes from the big screen and reappears on a four-and-a-half-inch silver disc (which it has, four months after release). But my long-suffering wife calls to me from the kitchen—"Finish it, would you, please?" and she's right, as usual. If I'm not careful, I'm going to wind up with too many climaxes, as in the last of Jackson's *The Lord of the Rings* trilogy, so it ends—now!

IF YOU ENJOYED THIS BOOK
PLEASE CALL, WRITE OR E-MAIL
FOR A FREE CATALOG

MIDNIGHT MARQUEE PRESS
9721 BRITINAY LANE
BALTIMORE, MD 21234

WWW.MIDMAR.COM
410-665-1198
MMARQUEE@AOL.COM

www.ingramcontent.com/pod-product-compliance
Lightning Source LLC
Chambersburg PA
CBHW050202130526
44591CB00034B/1869